Men Mentoring Men

Revised Edition

Men's Discipleship Course

**An Interactive One-on-One or Small Group
Christian Growth Manual for Men**

Daryl G. Donovan

CSS Publishing Company, Inc.
Lima, Ohio

MEN MENTORING MEN
REVISED EDITION

Copyright © 2014 by
CSS Publishing Company, Inc.
Lima, Ohio

Scripture quotations are from the New American Standard Bible, © 1960, 1962, 1963, 1968, 1971, 1972, 1973, 1975, 1977 by The Lockman Foundation. Used by permission.

Revised and reprinted edition from *Men Mentoring Men*, ISBN 0-7880-1184-7, printed in 1998 by CSS Publishing Company.

For more information about CSS Publishing Company resources, visit our website at www.csspub.com, email us at csr@csspub.com, or call (800) 241-4056.

e-book:
ISBN-13: 978-0-7880-2776-5
ISBN-10: 0-7880-2776-X

ISBN-13: 978-0-7880-2775-8
ISBN-10: 0-7880-2775-1

PRINTED IN USA

Men Mentoring Men
is dedicated
to the ones who have taught me most
about life, love, and living out the Christian faith...
my family:
Elaine, my wife, and our four wonderful children:
Rebekah, Kristen, Benjamin, and Kay

And to every man who desires to
follow Jesus, growing in him,
willing to make disciples.

Foreword

Scholars are one thing, students another, but a disciple is best of all.

The true principle of perpetuity in discipleship is to teach,
to teach, to teach.
The difference in quality of leadership is not in knowing how to do
something, but it is knowing why.

Israel saw God's acts; Moses knew God's ways.
It's the difference between followers and leaders.

In this discipleship course you are taken beyond the facts of doing into
the realm of being — being a "real man," that is.

All God wants is for you to be a man. That's what he created you to be —
nothing more, nothing less.

To learn to be a "real man" is to learn to be like Jesus.
Manhood and Christlikeness are synonymous.

The entire purpose of the teaching of Dr. Donovan is to take you
step-by-step into the stature of really mature manhood.

Everything in life is lived on levels and arrived at in stages.
This course can take you from your present stage
to a new level of manliness.

God bless you as you grow in grace and in the knowledge of the
Lord Jesus Christ!

Edwin Louis Cole
President/Founder
Christian Men's Network

Introduction

"And Jesus came up and spoke to them, saying, 'All authority has been given to me in heaven and on earth. Go therefore and make disciples of all the nations, baptizing them in the name of the Father and the Son and the Holy Spirit, teaching them to observe all that I commanded you; and lo, I am with you always, even to the end of the age.' "
Matthew 28:18-20

For the next several weeks we will be walking out the Great Commission. Jesus said to "make disciples." The purpose of this course is to help both the leader and the student to grow in their relationship with Jesus Christ. God's principle of "iron sharpening iron" will be evident.

Be diligent both in your attendance as well as in the completion of assignments. At the conclusion of this course you will be a "disciple-maker." You will have the tools and training to disciple another man into maturity in Christ.

Table of Contents

Session 1

What's This All About?

(Purpose and overview)

Purpose

(Why Are We Doing This?)

Jesus was continually about the business of making disciples. He taught and modeled the principles of the kingdom of God before his followers. He fully understood the value of investing in lives. What he did is precisely what he calls us to do: Make disciples!

A disciple is a learner... or follower. A disciple is one who adheres to a particular discipline. Christian disciple-making is encouraging, teaching, and nurturing others in the principles of the kingdom of God.

In these sessions together we will be considering how to be effective disciple-makers, as well as being equipped with the tools to do disciple-making. This course will be academic, but more than that, it will be relational. It is not a study to be done alone, but with another man or other men. While it will include great amounts of information, it will also include prayer support, accountability, and genuine Christian love and concern for one another.

The primary purpose of this course is growth in Jesus Christ. Both the discipler and the one being discipled will grow. As we grow, we will bear good fruit and our Father will be glorified (Matthew 5:16). Many individuals after becoming Christians fail to grow and discover all that God has in store for them. Sometimes it is because they do not realize the full potential God has for them. Often growth is hindered because other Christians fail to see the need or responsibility to nurture a new Christian. For too long we have been content with making converts instead of disciples.

Men Mentoring Men is about growth. It is about taking discipleship seriously. For the next several weeks we will walk together, work together, and grow together in the power of Jesus Christ... all to the glory of his name!

The Plan

(So What's Going To Happen?)

Our course of action is simple and measurable. The thrust of this course has four primary components. Please be faithful to the plan.

1. We will meet: We will meet regularly at an appointed time and place. We will meet for a designated amount of time. Extension of time or other meeting opportunities are negotiable. As we meet:
• Please be on time.
• Please give notice if you must miss.
• Catch up on materials in the event you must miss a session.

2. We will study: Always bring your Bible and *Men Mentoring Men* book. There will be regular assignments almost every week. Complete those assignments prior to the appointed meeting time.

3. We will pray: We will take time to pray for one another. Beyond our regular meeting time, we will serve as prayer partners, daily being lifted up in prayer.

4. We will be accountable: You will be called upon during the sessions together to share insights gleaned while doing your homework. If you miss a session without giving prior notification, you can expect a call. We give permission to each other to speak into one another's lives as we see areas of concern.

Please Note: Accountability is mutual — it works both ways. All involved will be called into account, including the leader. Accountability is not intrusive. It is with permission and will be graciously applied. Accountability is concern, not control. God is the one changing us... let's give him plenty of room to do so... in his time.

The Possibilities

(A Bold New Horizon)

Men Mentoring Men is about *life* — it is about *growth*! God's presence and his pleasure are always evident when men commit to surrender — to be available to be about the "Father's business." When you put together the combination of the working of our awesome, living, loving, powerful God... with a surrendered, pliable, teachable heart... the possibilities are limitless!

1. We will experience changed lives: The twelve men who walked with Jesus were never the same after meeting up with him. As we meet with one another, with Jesus in our midst, we will be changed.

* * *

A TESTIMONY

Bill was a brand-new Christian. His previous spiritual experience consisted of a journey from atheism to New Age philosophies. Jesus touched him profoundly and Bill surrendered his life to Christ.

Where did Bill go from there? He had fire flowing through his veins to grow in Christ. Bill called our church and asked, "I've become a Christian... now what do I do?" I said, "Let's get together."

For one year Bill and I met to discuss many topics. Boy, did he have questions! We studied the Bible. We prayed for one another. I watched this young man grow in leaps and bounds as Jesus met in our midst. Bill grew as a husband... as a father... and as a spiritual leader in the church and community. Why? Because of a teachable heart... a willing disciple... and the faithfulness of Jesus working in us.

* * *

We will experience changed lives as we proceed for the next several weeks.

2. We will foster deep, eternal relationships: When I was seventeen, a man told me that at the end of my life I would be able to count my "true" friends on one hand. I argued with him. Now I see his insight. Throughout our lives we will experience very few deep, lasting relationships. As we walk through this endeavor together, I believe God will do a "heart knitting" that will be profound... and eternal.

The relationships we will build will be tools of transformation in the hands of our loving Father... to conform us to the image of his Son.

3. We will be about the business of reaching our world according to biblical mandate: Jesus gave a commission to disciples standing around him nearly 2,000 years ago and that commission is passed on to us... his modern disciples.

> "Go therefore and make disciples of all the nations,
> baptizing them in the name of the Father and the Son
> and the Holy Spirit, teaching them to observe all that
> I commanded you; and lo, I am with you always,
> even to the end of the age."
> Matthew 28:19-20

In the Great Commission found recorded here in the gospel of Matthew, Jesus gave us his strategy for reaching the world. We have misunderstood this commission of Christ to mean that we should go and make converts. He was interested in the making of disciples. Disciples are men and women who are committed followers and learners who would impact their world.

With our passion to make converts we have failed to see the value of making disciples. Jesus proposed the perfect plan to reach the world. Disciple-making, one person at a time, is a far more effective way to see the kingdom of God expanded. Allow me to illustrate.

* * *

If I were to commit to meet with a man for one year, studying together, praying together, walking in accountability, we would both grow and be strengthened. At the end of that year, I would release him to disciple another man, and I seek a new disciple myself. At the end of two years we have three new disciples. Having encouraged, trained, and equipped these men, we all four venture to disciple four new men. At the end of three years, seven new disciples have been nurtured in Christ.

Now watch this...

At the end of ten years we will have 1,024 disciples....

At the end of fifteen years we will have 32,768 disciples....

At the end of twenty years we will have 1,048,576 disciples....

At the end of thirty years we will have

Over one billion disciples!

(This numerical illustration was given on the audio training series for "Training Faithful Men," Institute in Basic Life Principles.)

* * *

We do not have converts. These are not "pew warmers" on some membership roll. These are men and women who understand prayer, Bible study, witnessing... who are committed to spiritual growth. **Didn't Jesus have a great plan? ... and it still works!**

Walking This Out...

For 23 years I have been mentoring men, sometimes using this book... often simply meeting around the scriptures. Rarely do I meet one-on-one, but have done so occasionally. Usually our group includes 3 or 4 men... sometimes as many as 24. (We break up into smaller groups if that many come.)

Generally I meet with men in the morning, often for breakfast or over coffee. That time interferes least with family commitments and work. Sometimes those sessions are early.

Our times together include several elements:
1. We catch up, sharing for a few moments what is going on in our lives.
2. If it is appropriate, we sing a worship song or read a psalm. We often meet in a private area of a restaurant or a home.
3. We pray.
4. While we share the meal, we discuss the assigned reading or the scriptures.
5. We conclude with praying for one another.

Men Mentoring Men is fourteen sessions, but I often continue meeting with men beyond that. We may agree to a book of the Bible or a popular book for men to study together. I do however encourage the men to reach out to other men as we wrap up the fourteen sessions together.

Do you need a leader's guide? You have it in your hand. *Men Mentoring Men* is for both the discipler and the disciple. After all, you both are learning and growing in this process. You can supplement the material if you like, but I think it will give you plenty to discuss and consider. You will find many "bolded" questions that you should consider... and I am sure others will arise as you make your way through the material. Enjoy the journey together.

Assignment for Next Time

In our next session we will discuss, "Who we are in Christ." The Bible says that we have become a new creation (2 Corinthians 5:17). We are under "new management" as we surrender to Jesus Christ. Read all of Session 2 and be prepared to answer the bolded questions together. Meanwhile, pray for your mentoring partner(s).

Session 2

So What's New?

(Who we are in Christ)

So What's New?

One of the greatest crises in the Body of Christ today is that Christians don't fully realize who they are in Christ. Due to lack of knowledge or failure to understand, many Christians miss out on the "abundant life" Jesus freely offers. It is time to learn so that we might walk in confidence in Christ and be effective instruments for him.

We will consider several spiritual realities that Christianity affords us. As we discuss each item, seek to know each of these truths for yourself. *Why?* Because they are true for you... and as you walk in that truth you will experience the fullness God desires for you!

Spiritual Reality #1:
You are loved!

John 3:16: "For God so loved the world, that he gave his only begotten Son, that whoever believes in him should not perish, but have eternal life."

Romans 5:8: "But God demonstrates his own love toward us, in that while we were yet sinners, Christ died for us."

Ephesians 2:4-5: "But God, being rich in mercy, because of his great love with which he loved us, even when we were dead in our transgressions, made us alive together with Christ (by grace you have been saved)."

Love is an ambiguous word in our English language. We love pizza, our dog, a good joke, our children, our wife... and of course, God. In the Greek language, however, words are more precise. There are several words for love that better define the different levels of love. When we read in scripture of the love God has for us, the Greek word is *agape*. (That word is never used in reference to pizza!) It denotes both unconditional and sacrificial love. Romans 5:8 and John 3:16 both make it clear that God's love comes to us "while we were yet sinners" (unconditionally) and at a dear price, "He gave his only begotten Son" (sacrificially).

It wasn't until I had a son of my own that I fully appreciated God's sacrificial gift. I would lay down my own life for just about anyone, but I would not give up my son for anyone! God so loved us that he gave his only Son! Wow! Now that is love!

Do you grasp the reality that God loves you?

Spiritual Reality #2:
You are forgiven!

1 John 1:9: "If we confess our sins, he is faithful and righteous to forgive us our sins and to cleanse us from all unrighteousness."

Colossians 2:13-14: "And when you were dead in your transgressions and the uncircumcision of your flesh, he made you alive together with him, having forgiven us all our transgressions, having canceled out the certificate of debt consisting of decrees against us and which was hostile to us; and he has taken it out of the way, having nailed it to the cross."

Hebrews 10:12: "But he (Jesus), having offered one sacrifice for sins for all time, sat down at the right hand of God."

Knowing the reality of God's forgiveness is tough for many Christians. A man told me once that God casts our sins into the sea of forgetfulness and then puts up a sign that says, "No fishing!" But often we want to fish them back. We revive and relive the guilt of some past sins over and over again.

Not only do we struggle with the guilt of past sins (sins already forgiven and wiped clean by the blood of Jesus Christ), but we struggle with the *shame*. I have heard many men say, "Oh sure, I understand that I am forgiven... but I am so ashamed!"

Jesus bore not only our sin... he bore our shame. He hung naked on that cross, shamed by his enemies. You can know that not only has Christ dealt with your sin... he has dealt with your shame. The Apostle Paul, who once was a persecutor of Christians, could not have been the powerful servant of Christ if he had not understood that both the sin of his misdeeds and the *shame* of the suffering he had caused others had been fully satisfied by the redemptive work of Christ on the cross.

Have you fully embraced God's forgiveness?

Spiritual Reality #3:
You are a new creation!

2 Corinthians 5:17: "Therefore if any man is in Christ, he is a new creature; the old things passed away; behold, new things have come."

Galatians 2:20: "I have been crucified with Christ; and it is no longer I who live, but Christ lives in me; and the life which I now live in the flesh I live by faith in the Son of God, who loved me, and delivered himself up for me."

Wow! Something brand new has happened in your life. You are now under new management. Jesus has moved in and is working in your heart. You may not feel different — you may not even notice a big difference in your thoughts or actions right away, but you will. And it will be wonderful. **You are a new creation!**

The "newness" you are experiencing is brought to you by Jesus Christ. It is not something you "mustered up"! Let me assure you, as you continue to pursue a life of surrender to Christ, you will see his newness more and more.

Caution: Don't measure your newness by comparing yourself to others. Do not rely upon the testimonies of others to validate your experience with Jesus Christ. He deals with each of us uniquely. Saul, who was later known as the Apostle Paul, saw a flash of light in the desert and was radically converted. Peter met Jesus by the sea and simply began to follow him. Thomas came to know Christ through questions and proofs. Just because the newness you have experienced with Christ may not be as dramatic as the experiences of others, nor as emotional as some, it is just as valid. Jesus works his newness in many creative manifestations. Just be assured that if you are in Christ, and Christ is in you... you are a new creation!

What "new thing" stands out most to you after coming to Christ?

Reality #4:
You are being transformed.

> **Romans 12:2:** "And do not be conformed to this world, but be transformed by the renewing of your mind, that you may prove what the will of God is, that which is good and acceptable and perfect."

> **Philippians 3:12:** "Not that I have already obtained it, or have already become perfect, but I press on in order that I may lay hold of that for which also I was laid hold of by Christ Jesus."

We are a new creation in Christ. Much is new now that Christ lives in us. We are also *becoming* new. There is a process going on in our lives of being conformed to the image of Christ (Romans 8:29). We are being changed. Romans 12 says that we are being transformed!

The Greek word for transform is *metamorphei*. Think of that fuzzy worm, secure in the cocoon, being transformed (metamorphosis) into a beautiful butterfly. You are secure in the person of Jesus Christ, being transformed into his own likeness.

Be patient in this process. Often we become frustrated with our weaknesses — and with how slowly the change comes about.

* * *

> Several years ago, while returning from a pastors' conference, I was having a pity party. I was weeping and telling God how I hated my weaknesses. I wanted him to remove them all and make me like the speakers I had just heard. (See anything wrong with this picture?) As I prayed, I sensed the Lord saying to me, "If you did not have these weaknesses, you would not know how much you need me. You would be self-reliant and proud." I will *never* forget those words.

* * *

I have learned since that time not only to be patient about God's "change" process, but also to be grateful for my weaknesses.

Let me say, however, that while God does allow weakness in our lives for his purposes, he does not tolerate sin. Some men justify a repetitive sin in their life with words like, "Oh, that's just my weakness." For example, one may have the *weakness* of being *tempted* (temptation is not sin) to be involved with pornography. God will meet you in that weakness with sufficient grace and power to grow you through those temptations. However, to succumb to that temptation is *sin*, not *weakness*. We must flee from sin and come to Christ to receive his cleansing work. God's strength is perfected in our weakness (2 Corinthians 12:9). Not in our sin!

As Christ renews our hearts and our minds we find many of those weaknesses diminish or even disappear. We begin to discover the reality of "no longer being slaves to sin" (Romans 6). He is changing us every day to be more like Christ.

Name a weakness (one that perhaps may lead to sin) that is a struggle for you.

Spiritual Reality #5:
We have hope!

John 16:33: "These things I have spoken to you, that in me you may have peace. In the world you have tribulation, but take courage; I have overcome the world."

Romans 5:3-5: "And not only this, but we also exult in our tribulations, knowing that tribulation brings about perseverance; and perseverance, proven character; and proven character, hope; and hope does not disappoint, because the love of God has been poured out within our hearts through the Holy Spirit who was given to us."

Ephesians 2:12-13: "Remember that you were at that time separate from Christ, excluded from the commonwealth of Israel, and strangers to the covenants of promise, having no hope and without God in the world. But now in Christ Jesus you who formerly were far off have been brought near by the blood of Christ."

I have met so many depressed, discouraged Christians. So many Christians full of anxiety. One woman I knew worried constantly... about what others thought... about her health... her finances... about everything. She was a nervous wreck. Yet she was a Christian. One thing I noticed was that she had absolutely no witness for Christ. She was ineffective because she did not reflect the peace, power, and *hope* that Christ instills in our hearts.

We are told in God's word that once we had no hope. We were on a road to eternal destruction, apart from God... but now... we are destined for eternal life in Christ! Death does not defeat us! Paul told the Thessalonians not to grieve as those who have no hope (1 Thessalonians 4:13). We will grieve even as Christians, but not a hopeless grief. We know that God has a wonderful eternal picture for all who have called upon the name of Jesus in faith.

Not only do we have hope for the eternal future, we have hope even in our tribulations. God really does cause all things to work together for good for those who love him and are called according to his purposes (Romans 8:28). Yes, we will have trials and struggles in life, but Jesus reminded us to "be of good courage"!

We also have hope because we do not bear our burdens alone. We are to cast all our cares on him because he does care for us (1 Peter 5:7). He will grant to us all the comfort we need in our times of loss or sorrow if we will turn to him (2 Corinthians 1:3-4). Oh, the wonderful hope... the assurance we have in Christ.

Finally, we have hope for the eternal destiny of the world and the human race. Polls show that many people are anxious about the economy... anxious about the future. Let me assure you, the one who has written the final chapter of history from the foundation of the world has penned a triumphant "happy ending" for those who know him. Be full of hope!

Are you a hope-filled follower of Jesus?

Spiritual Reality #6:
We are empowered.

Luke 11:13: "If you then, being evil, know how to give good gifts to your children, how much more shall your heavenly Father give the Holy Spirit to those who ask him?"

Ephesians 5:18: "And do not get drunk with wine, for that is dissipation, but be filled with the Spirit."

We will spend an entire session on the person of the Holy Spirit. For now, however, simply be reminded that we are empowered to be witnesses for Christ and effective instruments for God's purposes.

We have the Holy Spirit enabling us to "be all that we can be" in Christ. He comes, as promised by Jesus, to convict us of sin, and prompt us to do right (John 16:8). He will give us boldness to live a life that reflects Jesus to the world (Acts 1:8). He will bring gifts, truly tools, to accomplish his purposes. He will bear fruit in our lives that we are absolutely incapable of bearing on our own (John 15:5).

Let me ask at this point: Have you surrendered to let the Holy Spirit have full control in your life? A real key to experiencing the fullness of the Holy Spirit's work is fully submitting to him. Ask God to fill you with the Holy Spirit. In Ephesians where Paul gives the command to be filled with the Holy Spirit, the command is in the present active tense. That means the words are literally, "keep on being filled." We need to daily seek God to fill us with the Holy Spirit.

How is your tank today?

Spiritual Reality #7:
We are people of purpose!

Matthew 5:48: "Therefore you are to be perfect, as your heavenly Father is perfect."

Philippians 1:21: "For to me, to live is Christ, and to die is gain."

Colossians 1:9: "For this reason also, since the day we heard of it, we have not ceased to pray for you and to ask that you may be filled with the knowledge of his will in all spiritual wisdom and understanding."

Why are you here on the planet? If you were to die at this moment, for what would you be remembered? What "mark" have you made on the world? What would the preacher say at your funeral?

As people of God, we are people with purpose. Paul told the Colossian Christians that they had great faith... and lots of love... and that he would fervently pray for them to fully know God's will. It is so crucial that we know what to do with our lives and with all that God has granted to us. Too many people, including many Christians, wander aimlessly through life, wondering why they are here.

Have you ever struggled with the verse quoted above from Matthew's gospel about "being perfect"? I used to read that verse, assume it was impossible... then read on. Let me give you something to consider.

In the Greek language the words *perfect* and *purpose* share the same root meaning. There is a connection between being perfect and knowing your purpose. Let me explain.

* * *

A few years ago I was bravely attempting to be a handyman, working on our plumbing, of all things! I needed a screwdriver, so I called to my wife to please bring me one. She brought me a regular, flat screwdriver. I needed a Phillips head. I told my wife my dilemma and she graciously went and exchanged the flat screwdriver for a Phillips head. I placed the screwdriver on the head of the screw and exclaimed, "Now that's perfect!" Even though the screwdriver was rusty, bent, and splotched with paint, it was fulfilling its designed purpose.

* * *

You were designed for a purpose. You may have wrinkles, weaknesses, scars... all kinds of "imperfections," but you still have the capacity to walk in the perfection of his will... his designed purpose for your life. As you discover and walk in his will you will find great joy and fulfillment in your life.

Throughout the course of *Men Mentoring Men* knowing God's will is a high priority. Have faith and courage to walk in his will... and you will enjoy the godly perfection Jesus was talking about... and that Paul was praying for the Colossians ... and you!

Write your own personal "purpose statement."

In Conclusion

We have only scratched the surface of who we are in Christ. Jesus meant it when he said the life he gives is abundant. Be encouraged. Walk in the fullness he has for you. Do not allow the lies of men or of Satan to rob you of all that God has for you.

> "The thief comes only to steal, and kill, and destroy; I came that they might have life, and might have it abundantly."
> John 10:10

Walking This Out...

While Christ has made us new, we are all in process. Billy Graham's wife, Ruth, had this epitaph put on her tombstone: "Construction Complete... thank you for your patience." We are not done until we are done here.

As I walk this walk with other men I regularly remind them of who they are in Christ. I encourage and challenge them with the good news that we are being transformed.

To keep myself on that intentional growth track, there are several steps I take:
1. I maintain a consistent quiet time of prayer and meditation on

scripture.

2. I stay in close relationship with other men who hold me accountable and encourage me to be more in Christ.

3. I make every effort to stay in tune with the Holy Spirit's conviction, quick to confess sin and to repent.

4. I carefully guard what my ears hear and what my eyes see… and where I allow my thoughts to go.

5. I strive to maintain healthy relationships, avoiding taking offenses, ready to forgive and restore.

We don't grow accidentally, men! Feed and water the seed God has planted in you. Press on!

Next Session

In our next session we will begin to discuss the Bible. We will look at some history (such as how we got our Bible and why it is absolutely reliable). We will talk about how to study the Bible and how to read the Bible devotionally.

Session 3

Walking In The Word

(The Bible, my blueprint)

Walking In The Word

In this session, we will consider what it means to be men of the word. The Bible is God's wonderful "blueprint" given to show us how to build our lives upon Christ. It is a lamp shining upon the path of life so that we might stay on course. The psalmist wrote, "Thy word is a lamp to my feet, and a light to my path" (Psalm 119:105).

Jesus stressed the vital importance of being people who walk according to the word of God. In fact, he said it was a mark of being a disciple:

> **John 8:31-32:** "If you abide in my word, then you are truly disciples of mine; and you shall know the truth and the truth shall make you free."

Men Mentoring Men is about being disciples. We are learners, followers... students of Jesus Christ. Since we truly are his disciples, we truly will be men who abide in his word.

We will consider how the Bible came to be and why it is absolutely reliable as the inspired, inerrant Word of God. We will discuss the difference between reading the Bible devotionally and reading it analytically (as a study). Finally, why is it important to be saturated in the Word of God? Why did Jesus put such an emphasis upon abiding in the Word? In the appendix you will find a list of resources for your own devotional reading and Bible study.

Bible Backgrounds

How the Bible came to be.

There is no other book like the Bible! At least forty different authors had a hand in the writing of the Bible over a period of more than 1,500 years. It is incredible in scope, astounding in accuracy, and remarkable in consistency! Even with the input of so many writers over so many years, there are no contradictions or errors. Indeed, it is a "holy" book... one of a kind!

The Bible holds its distinction as a unique book because it is *inspired* of the Holy Spirit. The words penned on the pages of the Bible were authored by men who were attuned to the Great Author, recording events, teachings, and testimonies as God directed. What does it mean to say that the Bible is inspired by the Holy Spirit? I agree with Charles Ryrie in his definition of biblical inspiration:

> *"Biblical inspiration is God's superintendence of the human authors so that, using their own individual personalities, they composed and recorded without error his revelation to man in the words of the original autographs."*

Inspiration does not mean that God dictated the words *verbatim*, but that he directed the authors as they accurately penned his truth. Therefore, scriptures will reflect historical influences, as well as author personality and perspective. In other words, John's perspective varies from that of Matthew as they write about the life of Jesus, yet both are absolutely accurate and precise in writing what God wanted written. Fully inspired of God, the writings of Peter and Paul reflect personalities that were quite different. It is amazing to see how God has mixed all of the various influences in the development of a book that flows so beautifully, speaks so powerfully, and proclaims so accurately his truth for life here on planet earth and for the life to come!

What's the test of accuracy?

Volumes have been written about God's involvement in human history. Teachings and truths have been proclaimed often with the claim of "inspiration." Not all of these writings, however, have been included in the Bible, nor are they regarded with the same level of authority. Who decided what got in the Bible and what did not — and by what measure did they decide?

In a nutshell (it would take volumes to tell the whole story), the discussion of which books belong in the Bible is the question of canon. Canon is a "measuring rod," not some huge gun. All of the writings regarded as scripture today have stood the test of time and careful scrutiny by the church. Over the centuries many councils of Christians have gathered to study, evaluate, and verify biblical authenticity. The Holy Spirit was an operative in the process of canonization as well as the writing of scriptures.

The writings underwent several tests:

1. The content had to reflect accuracy and uniqueness, clearly portraying revelation from God.

2. Authorship had to be reputable. Old Testament prophets always had to be right or their writings did not make it. New Testament writers had to have apostolic sanction to be considered authoritative as scripture.

3. The church, often through gatherings of councils, recognized the authenticity and authority of the manuscripts and gave approval to canonization.

Failure to pass any one of these tests would eliminate writings from the biblical canon. While the scriptures have been copied several times over the centuries, they were copied with detailed accuracy. That accuracy has been confirmed with the discoveries of ancient manuscripts. Today we have over 24,000 manuscripts of the New

Testament that attest to the careful transference of the biblical record.

If you simply compare the Bible to other historical documents, based on number of copies, and how close those copies are to the original, the Bible stands head and shoulders above the rest when it comes to reliability. Consider the following chart:

Author	No. of Copies	Time Span
Caesar	10	1,000 years
Plato (Tetralogies)	7	1,200 years
Tacitus (Annals)	20	1,000 years
Pliny the Younger (History)	7	750 years
Suetonius (De Vita Caesarum)	8	800 years
Homer (Iliad)	643	500 years
New Testament	Over 24,000	25 years

(Chart from Christian Apologetics and Research Ministry: CARM.org)

Paul wrote to Timothy:

> **2 Timothy 3:16-17:** "All scripture is inspired by God and profitable for teaching, for reproof, for correction, for training in righteousness; that the man of God may be adequate, equipped for every good work."

How reliable do you consider the Bible to be?

So What Do We Do With This Book?

We read it! We choose a translation that works well for us (you may want to consult with your pastor about different translations), and we begin to devour God's word. But there are several different ways to read the Bible.

Casual Reading:

Hebrews 4:12: "For the word of God is living and active and sharper than any two-edged sword, and piercing as far as the division of soul and spirit, of both joints and marrow, and able to judge the thoughts and intentions of the heart."

The word of God is powerful even when we casually expose ourselves to it. I like to keep a Bible handy in the car, the bathroom (hey, I can mention that with *men*), or any other place where I might discover a few moments just to "browse" through the word. I also have the Bible on my iPad and iPhone and whenever I have down time, I listen to or read scripture. While this is not devotional reading, and certainly not Bible study, it still has powerful, positive effects.

What opportunities do you have for casual reading of the Bible?

Devotional Reading:

Psalm 1:1-2: "How blessed is the man who does not walk in the counsel of the wicked, nor stand in the path of sinners, nor sit in the seat of scoffers! But his delight is in the law of the Lord and in his law he meditates day and night."

Devotional reading is meditating on the word of God. Typically it is when you have time to get quiet for a few moments and allow God to speak to you through his word. It usually does not consist of reading great amounts of scripture, but focusing on a few verses.

During devotional Bible reading moments it is wise to pray prior to reading, inviting God to reveal what he has for you in the verses you are about to read. You may want to use a devotional guide or Bible reading plan or randomly read through scriptures. (Usually I have a Bible reading plan.) When I am not using a reading plan, I often turn to Psalms or Proverbs. After reading the verses, simply sit quietly and ponder what the Lord might be saying to you. In your journal, write reflections on the verses you have read. Many times when a verse has a personal pronoun, or spiritual quality, I will put my name in that place and reflect on the impact those words have for me.

Try that now. Meditate on 1 Corinthians 13:4-7.

1 Corinthians 13:4-7: "Love is patient, love is kind, and is not jealous; love does not brag and is not arrogant, does not act unbecomingly, it does not seek its own, is not provoked, does not take into account a wrong suffered, does not rejoice in unrighteousness, but rejoices with the truth."

As you meditated on these verses, what thoughts did you have? What spoke to you personally? Try personalizing these verses by putting your name each time the word "love" appears or is implied.

Devotionally Through
The Bible In One Year

Reading through the whole Bible is a good devotional plan. You can do that straight through or follow a variable plan. Three to four chapters a day will get you through the Bible in about one year. In the supplements of many Bibles is a reading schedule to complete the whole Bible in one year.

Have you ever read through the entire Bible? If so, tell how it went for you. If not, would you be willing to give it a try? What might be some "drawbacks" for you in taking on the plan to read the Bible all the way through?

Bible Study:

Bible study is more than just reading scripture. Study is carefully reading the scriptures, consulting with academic resources, considering historical information as well as language usage to go deeper with the text.

When I meet with men for Bible study, I encourage them in what I call a simplified inductive method. Inductive study means taking a look at the verse from many angles.

First we just read the verses carefully and note any questions that arise, words that are repeated, a main theme that is arising. We give attention to every word.

Second, we consider the context. What came before and what comes after, and how it fits in the whole Bible story. A good reference Bible will show in the margin other passages in the Bible that are related to the text. The Bible is often the best commentary on the Bible. We ask the questions who, what, where, when, and why.

Hesitantly, we next turn to commentaries and other study guides. It is good first to ask what the Holy Spirit is saying to you through this text before you read what someone else has discerned.

So what are some helpful study tools?

Commentaries are valuable for Bible study. A commentary consists of others "comments" on the text. I prefer commentaries that are a "team" project put together by several scholars rather than by just one person. The approach is usually more balanced. There are, however, some excellent single-author commentaries. You will find a brief list of available references for your Bible study in the appendix.

A concordance is a productive tool for biblical research. Usually your Bible will have a concordance somewhere in the final pages. A concordance helps you find words or topics in scripture. For example, if you want to find every verse in the Bible that mentions "sin," an *exhaustive* concordance would list them all. There are free or inexpensive concordance applications for your computer and phone.

A Bible dictionary is helpful. What is a mite in biblical references? No, it is not a bug! It is a very small coin, in fact, the coin of very little value in Jesus' day. That is what the poor woman put in the temple offering and that was all she had. A Bible dictionary sheds helpful light on just how poor that woman was as she gave all.

Chain reference Bibles and study Bibles are good in that they serve as a "self-contained," condensed Bible study tool. Often you will find notes in the margins. Chain reference Bibles show how verses relate to one another.

Bible study is fun, exciting, and stimulating to our Christian growth. I am grateful for insights others have learned and passed on so that we might more fully understand the scriptures. It would be wise to check with your pastor as to recommended tools for your Bible research.

Our inductive study would not be complete if we did not then ask ourselves: "So what is the main point God wanted us to get out of this passage?" Too often we can dance around the scripture and never get to just what the Bible is saying.

When we grasp that main point, we must ask ourselves: "What do I do with what I have learned?" The scriptures are for learning... and for living.

What tools do you use most often when you study the Bible?

Memorization:

> **Psalm 119:11:** "Thy word I have treasured in my heart, that I may not sin against thee."

There may come a day when we do not have full access to the scriptures and only those verses we have memorized will be to what we cling. Even today, there are times I don't have my Bible handy, and I am grateful for those verses sown deep in my heart and mind.

Memorization is not as hard as you may think. Try the above verse for next time.

In Conclusion

Isn't God's word wonderful? We truly are Christ's disciples as we resolve to abide in his word! As we abide we will see some great things take place:

• We will discover that the truth does set us free. We are bound by so many lies. God's truth will bring triumph to your life. The Holy Spirit will speak reproof and exhortation that will be life-giving to us as we read God's word (2 Timothy 3:16).
• We will find spiritual power and authority. Jesus sent Satan running when he quoted scripture to him. The Bible is our spiritual sword (Ephesians 6:17).
• We will see results in our witness. God's word never comes back empty (Isaiah 55:11). Our opinion may be wonderful, but it may be wonderfully wrong. Sharing God's *truth* rather than our opinions gives life!
• We will know the will of God. The Bible is a blueprint for life and God will use his word to light our path (Psalm 119:105).
• Our mind will be renewed (Romans 12:2). As we fill our thoughts with God's word a lot of "junk" will get flushed out!

> "If you abide in my word, then you are truly disciples of mine; and you shall know the truth and the truth shall make you free."
> John 8:31-32

Walking This Out...

The Bible is amazing! It is both a love letter and an instruction book at the same time. Jesus said his disciples are those who abide in his word. That means to be at home in the scriptures.

Here are a few things I do:

1. I read a short passage (perhaps only one verse) during my quiet time simply to meditate upon it. The journal I use has a daily verse to consider.

2. I stay involved in a Bible study. I am engaged in studies of other books, but there is no book like the Bible. A verse by verse inductive study is so enriching.

3. I read the entire Bible every few years. There are reading plans or you can just jump in at Genesis and read right through.

4. I practice the scriptures. If you just read it or hear it and don't do it, you will not bear fruit. Be ready to obey.

Walk in the word!

Next Session

Prayer is our focus next session. Jesus' disciples said, "Teach us to pray." There are principles of prayer we must understand to experience power in our prayer life. We will consider those principles next time.

Session 4

Passionate In Prayer

(Being a man of prayer)

Passionate In Prayer

Colossians 4:2: "Devote yourselves to prayer, keeping alert in it, with an attitude of thanksgiving."

We must be men of prayer to be effective instruments in the hand of God. Jesus, the great "discipler" of us all, was clearly a man of prayer:

Mark 1:35: "And in the early morning, while it was still dark, he arose and went out and departed to a lonely place, and was praying there."

Luke 5:16: "But he himself would often slip away to the wilderness to pray."

Luke 6:12: "And it was at this time that he went off to the mountain to pray, and he spent the whole night in prayer to God."

Will we follow him to a lonely place — a quiet place to spend time in prayer? If Jesus Christ, the very Son of God, *often* spent quality quiet time with the Father, it seems safe to conclude that we would need the same.

A survey was done of 100 pastors asking them how much time, on average, they spent in prayer each day. This did not include public or pastoral prayers. The average response among the 100 pastors was "less than three minutes." Could it be that much of the struggle the church engages today relates directly to our unwillingness to be alone with God and pray?

47

How much time per day do you involve yourself in conversations with God?

Devoted To Prayer

The Apostle Paul understood the priority of prayer, continuing to call Christians to passionately pursue the Father, just as Jesus had done. In fact, Paul called us to be devoted to prayer. What is devotion?

* * *

> Devotion: 1. profound dedication; consecration. 2. earnest attachment to a cause, person, etc.... 3. The ready will to perform that which belongs to the service of God.
> (Random House Unabridged Dictionary of the English Language)

* * *

Being devoted to prayer is not a casual commitment. It is dedicated discipline to spend time in earnest communication with the Creator of the universe.

Devotion to prayer has the result of spiritual alertness in our lives. You see, prayer is not just "talking to God." Prayer is communication. Communication involves listening. As we foster an intimate disciplined "prayer life" we will be alert to what God is saying and doing in his world today. We will be alert to hear the answers to the questions we are asking.

Being devoted to prayer also promotes an attitude of thanksgiving. I have never met a man who daily spent quality quiet times with God who was a grumbler! Prayer impacts our lives in such a way that we are grateful for God's care for us. He is the living God who listens and speaks to those who seek him.

Teach Us To Pray

Luke 11:1: "And it came about that while he was praying in a certain place, after he had finished, one of his disciples said to him, 'Lord, teach us to pray just as John also taught his disciples.'"

Jesus' disciples wanted to know how to pray. They saw Jesus pray and they wanted to follow him. Therefore, they said, "Lord, teach us to pray." The verses that follow this request are often referred to as The Lord's Prayer. These verses contain principles and a pattern for prayer not to be neglected in our own prayer life. We find the Lord's Prayer in its fullest form in the gospel of Matthew 6:9-13. Let's take time to consider what Jesus was saying about prayer.

1. Prayer begins with praise.

Matthew 6:9: "Our Father, who art in heaven. Hallowed be thy name."

Begin your prayer time declaring the awesome holiness of God. Praise him! Tell him of your love for him. Have you noticed how the psalms are full of praise?

Let me encourage you to praise God as your Father. Jesus was very specific. He did not say, "Pray... dear God." He used the intimate, personal term of Father. When you pray, say, "Father." God is not your "good buddy up in the sky," nor is he some unreachable monarch... he is your heavenly Father.

2. Prayer continues with surrender.

Matthew 6:10: "Thy kingdom come, thy will be done, on earth as it is in heaven."

Often when I come to God in prayer I have my list of requests. When I submit to his will, however, many times I see that list shortened... or disappear. How often do we pray with our "answer running." We have only come to God for his stamp of approval rather than genuinely seeking his will. Be sure your requests line up with his kingdom principles.

* * *

A woman asked me once to pray that she would win the lottery. (I told her that I would pray that God would show her better ways to look to him for provision.)

A young man asked me to pray that his married girlfriend would divorce her husband so that he could marry her. (I told him I would pray that God would give him strength to repent and flee from this sinful relationship.)

* * *

I could not pray either of these prayer requests consistently with Matthew 6:10.

3. Look to God for daily provision.

Matthew 6:11: "Give us this day our daily bread."

Sorting our needs from our wants is a huge struggle we face daily. God is about the business of seeing to it that our daily needs are met. He also frequently blesses our wants. The problem is, we have trouble sorting out just what our needs are.

A real hindrance to prayer is being anxious about "things." We worry so much about finances and material possessions. Let's see what Jesus said about "things."

Matthew 6:31-33: "Do not be anxious then, saying, 'What

shall we eat?' or 'What shall we drink?' or 'With what shall we clothe ourselves?' For all these things the Gentiles eagerly seek; for your heavenly Father knows that you need all these things. But seek first his kingdom and his righteousness and all these things shall be added to you."

It is no accident that the request for daily bread *follows* the declaration "thy kingdom come, thy will be done." Ask God to help you sort needs from wants, and ask him to give to you your daily bread.

4. Fulfillment found in forgiveness.

Matthew 6:12: "Forgive us our debts, as we also have forgiven our debtors."

A bitter heart is clogged from hearing God. You can never enjoy a quality prayer life harboring unforgiveness. When you are not right in your relationship with others, you are not right in your relationship with God. God does not take unforgiveness lightly. In fact, this issue of unforgiveness is so important that Jesus came back to it at the conclusion of the prayer.

Matthew 6:14-15: "For if you forgive men for their transgressions, your heavenly Father will also forgive you. But if you do not forgive men, then your Father will not forgive your transgressions."

That's a heavy verse! (I've never seen it posted on anyone's refrigerator!) Unforgiveness stands in the way of our fully realizing the forgiveness of God for ourselves, therefore hindering prayer.

I strive to begin each day setting my heart *always* to forgive. You will be hurt, offended, and mistreated on a regular basis in this life. Will you choose to forgive? May I suggest that the forgiveness you give be unconditional. Do not expect people to admit what they have done to you. Do not require an apology. Do not develop a set of steps they must fulfill to earn your forgiveness. **Just forgive!** Unforgiveness will only diminish your life. Clearly Jesus taught that it would hinder your communication with God.

5. Look to God for triumph over temptation.

> **Matthew 6:13:** "And do not lead us into temptation, but deliver us from evil."

Does God lead us into temptation? I think he does. If he did not, why would Jesus say that we should ask God not to? I know that God tempts no man (James 1:13), but I believe that he leads us to testing places for us to learn spiritual lessons. God, by the Holy Spirit, led Jesus into a place of temptation:

> **Matthew 4:1:** "Then Jesus was led up by the Spirit into the wilderness to be tempted by the devil."

As Jesus was launched into his purpose and call as the sacrificial lamb of God, he encountered the "test" or "temptation" to use his power for other purposes. His very identity was called into question as Satan uttered the words, "If you are the Son of God...." Jesus triumphed through this test and faithfully fulfilled the call.

You and I will endure tests too. Jesus said, however, that we should pray that God not lead us into temptation or tests.

I think Jesus understood the difficulty of temptation. That was no artificial struggle with Satan in the wilderness. Jesus was genuinely tempted, just as we are. It was hard for him, and it is hard for us. Pray to God that we not be led into many of those encounters.

Second, I think Jesus told us to pray this prayer because God has a better way to teach us. Often I pray that God would teach me first through his word, by the Holy Spirit, rather than through tests. If we don't learn spiritual principles the "easy" way, God will help us learn them through tests.

6. Prayer concludes with praise.

> **Matthew 6:13:** "For thine is the kingdom, and the power, and the glory forever. Amen!"

Can you imagine how different your day would be if you began it praising God? If you rise up out of those quiet moments with him singing or shouting words of praise, you will be different and the world will see that you have spent time with your Father. You will be more like him as you have earnestly pursued his presence.

To what degree are the principles of The Lord's Prayer evidenced in your own prayer life?

Hearing God

Much has been written about hearing God. Prayer is communication that involves both speaking and listening. We must be quiet enough to hear him. We must become familiar with his voice to know when it is God speaking to us. Much has been said or done supposedly as a directive from God that clearly was not. We are to be wise, discerning, and alert in our prayers to hear and to know the voice of God.

Peter Lord, who wrote the book *Hearing God*, was instrumental in deepening my prayer life, teaching me how to focus in prayer... and more importantly, to hear God. At a conference on prayer, Dr. Lord encouraged us to go off in the woods alone and ask God what he would want to say to us. He suggested we journal our prayers (which does help with focus), including the responses we sense from God. Sitting on a log in the woods, after writing out my petitions to God I asked, "So God, what would you like to say to me this fine morning?" In my spirit I heard God say, "I would say, 'Good Morning'." Tears filled my eyes. I just heard my Father, my king, the Creator of the universe tell me good morning. I am convinced God wants that kind of intimate relationship with each of us. I hear him daily speak words of encouragement, correction, and direction.

In the Bible we find recorded many ways in which God has communicated with the human race. Because God has not changed, it seems likely that each of these avenues of communication is still possible today. God is a living, caring Father who is involved with his creation. He is still speaking through the Bible as well as other means.

Here are some biblical examples of how God has communicated:

The Bible	2 Timothy 3:16
Audible Voice	Acts 9:4
Anointed Sermons	Acts 2
Signs/Circumstances	Judges 6/Acts 5:12
Visions	Acts 9-10
Angels	Matthew 1:20/Acts 5, 8, and 12
Holy Spirit	John 16:13
Prophetic Utterance	Acts 21:10
The Church	Acts 6:3
Jesus Christ	Hebrews 1:1-2
Other Christians	Acts 9:17-18
Other (Balaam's donkey)	Numbers 22:30

How do we discern God's voice? How can we be sure the communication we have received is from God? There are several tools of discernment available to us as we seek to hear God.

Most importantly, any communication that seems to have come from God must not contradict the Bible. The Bible is a dependable "measuring rod" to assist in the validation of a communication from God.

Second, knowing the nature of God himself will clarify the origin of many messages. Does what you have heard or sensed line up with the character of God? When the insane man said that God told him to kill his wife and children, it did not take great insight to discern the voice that had spoken was not that of God. The command was against the character of God.

Third, God has given us spiritual leaders to submit to for counsel. Whenever I sense a prompting from God, I "bounce" it off of a couple of trusted Christian leaders for confirmation, clarification, or rejection.

A fourth test, and least valuable, is experientially. Do you have a "peace" with what you have sensed or heard? Is this experience of God's communication consistent with previous communications?

In practice, I take all four of these tests into consideration when I sense God's prompting. It is a serious matter to say one has heard from God. It is an equally serious matter to hear rightly and to respond appropriately.

How has God spoken to you?

In Conclusion

Men, we must be men of prayer! Jesus was a man of prayer and we are his disciples. We will not know what it means to stand as men until we get down on our knees!

Walking This Out...

I used to see prayer as an important part of the Christian walk. I now see it as the most important aspect of our walk with Jesus. Prayer is our connection with the living God.

Here are some prayer steps I take...

I begin the day with prayer. Before worldly things start to happen and distractions come, I go to the Father.

That first prayer is a prayer of surrender.

Praise and thanksgiving are interwoven in my prayers throughout the day.

I practice, the stop, drop, and pray method. I don't put off giving attention to a prayer request or need.

I listen when I pray and I always hear the Shepherd. I journal my prayers.

I respond to what I hear the Shepherd say.

I make every effort daily to maintain an attitude of prayer, keeping alert to the Holy Spirit.

For years prayer was a discipline. Now it is a delight!

Next Session

In our next session we will discuss what it means to walk in the power of the Holy Spirit. Why did God send the "helper"? What are the "gifts" of the Holy Spirit available to Christians, and what are they for? What is the fruit of the Holy Spirit? These are just some of the topics we will consider as we gather next time.

Session 5

Counting On The Coach

(The Spirit-led life)

Your Advantage

John 16:7-13: "But I tell you the truth, it is to your advantage that I go away; for if I do not go away, the helper shall not come to you; but if I go I will send him to you. And he, when he comes, will convict the world concerning sin, and righteousness, and judgment; concerning sin, because they do not believe in me; and concerning righteousness, because I go to the Father, and you no longer behold me; and concerning judgment because the ruler of this world has been judged. I have many more things to say to you, but you cannot bear them now. But when he, the Spirit of truth, comes, he will guide you into all the truth; for he will not speak on his own initiative, but whatever he hears, he will speak; and he will disclose to you what is to come."

In the game of tennis, when one of the players is in position to score the winning point, it is said to be his "advantage." It is sort of like that with what Jesus said about the Holy Spirit. If we "get the point" that Jesus would be sending the Holy Spirit, we will understand the advantage that is ours. As difficult as it must have been to see Jesus ascend back to the Father, the disciples must have found great encouragement in knowing that the Holy Spirit was on his way.

What advantage does the Holy Spirit bring to us?

1. Conviction of sin: The Holy Spirit whispers to our conscience when we have transgressed the will of God. Often after people first receive Christ they come under heavy conviction for various sins. They should not be discouraged. The Holy Spirit is merely doing his part in the process of transforming the new believer.

2. Conviction of righteousness: Not only does the Holy Spirit convict of sin, he also prompts us to do right. He convinces us of the right thing to do. Often we can sense the Holy Spirit encouraging us to be obedient to the word of God. He moves us on in Christlikeness.

3. Leading into all truth: Third, the Holy Spirit is the revealer of truth. The Holy Spirit is the one who reveals to the unbeliever — and to believers — the *truth* about Jesus. He even tells us what is to come. According to the Apostle Paul's letter to the Christians at Rome, the Holy Spirit is the one who reveals to us the truth of who we are. We know, by the Holy Spirit, that we are children of God (Romans 8:16).

How have you experienced the Holy Spirit at work in your life?

Help!

John 14:16-17: "And I will ask the Father, and he will give you another helper, that he may be with you forever; this is the Spirit of truth, whom the world cannot receive, because it does not behold him or know him, but you know him because he abides with you, and will be in you."

Luke 11:13: "If you then, being evil, know how to give good gifts to your children, how much more shall your heavenly Father give the Holy Spirit to those who ask him?"

Acts 2:38: "And Peter said to them, 'Repent, and let each of you be baptized in the name of Jesus Christ for the forgiveness of your sins; and you shall receive the gift of the Holy Spirit.'"

Every person who has surrendered his or her life to Christ has received the gift of the Holy Spirit. According to John 14, the Holy

Spirit comes as our helper. We need God's help to be all that we can be for him.

The word "helper" has rich meaning. It means comforter. The Holy Spirit comes to give supernatural courage in our times of human frailty. Because of him, we can have the peace that passes all under-standing.

Helper also means counselor. The Holy Spirit is our wise advisor. James told us if we lacked wisdom, to ask God for it. The Holy Spirit delivers wisdom to us as he comes to us as counselor.

The word "helper" was an athletic term in Jesus' day. It was the term used to define the role of the "coach." The Holy Spirit is our Holy Coach, encouraging, training, correcting, and enabling us to "play the game" to win. He keeps us focused and provides the game plan for us to cross the finish line with satisfaction. We must listen to the coach and we must obey if we are to achieve the prize!

How attentive are you to the guidance of the Holy Spirit as your coach?

Power Tools

Not only does the Holy Spirit bring to us wise counsel, comfort, and correction, he brings gifts to be used as tools to carry out his king-dom tasks. At least 26 gifts are mentioned in scripture:

Spiritual Gifts

Spiritual Gift	Scripture Reference
Administration	1 Corinthians 12:28
Apostolic Nurturing	Ephesians 4:11
Celibacy	1 Corinthians 14:13
Discernment	1 Corinthians 12:10
Evangelism	Ephesians 4:11
Exhortation	Romans 12:8
Exorcism	Acts 8:5-8

Faith	1 Corinthians 12:9
Giving	Romans 12:8
Healing	1 Corinthians 12:9
Helps	1 Corinthians 12:28
Hospitality	Romans 12:13
Intercession	Ephesians 6:18
Interpretation of Tongues	1 Corinthians 12:10
Knowledge	1 Corinthians 12:8
Leadership	Romans 12:8
Mercy	Romans 12:8
Miracles	1 Corinthians 12:10
Missionary	Acts 13:2-3
Pastor	Ephesians 4:11
Prophetic	Ephesians 4:11
Service	Romans 12:7
Speaking in Tongues	1 Corinthians 12:10
Teaching	Ephesians 4:11
Voluntary Poverty	1 Corinthians 13:1-3
Wisdom	1 Corinthians 12:8

(Condensed from: *Finding Your Spiritual Gifts*, Wagner-Modified Houts Questionnaire)

In 1 Corinthians 12:7 it says that "to each one is given the manifestation of the Spirit for the common good." In verse 11 Paul wrote, "But one and the same Spirit works all these things, distributing to each one individually just as he wills." Do you know how he has gifted you? It also says in 1 Corinthians 14:1 that we should "desire earnestly spiritual gifts." Paul is saying that we should desire God's tools, not for our own glory, but to be effective for the kingdom work given to us. Are you open to receive every spiritual gift God knows you need?

* * *

I had a young man tell me once that he wanted to be an instrument for God. He wanted to be all that God wanted him to be. He said that he had totally surrendered his life to Christ. In the next breath, however, he did say that he told God that he didn't want any of the weird stuff... any gifts that might embarrass him. I simply asked him, "Bill, are you really sure you have surrendered all?" Bill had put qualifiers on how he wanted God to move in his life.

* * *

Do you know what your spiritual gifts are?

Why Plug In?

I call the gifts of the Holy Spirit "power tools." They are divinely powerful tools that go beyond our human resources to get the job done. Why do we need them? Why is it essential that we plug in to God's power?

1. We can *only* get the job done by the power of the Holy Spirit. This is a spiritual endeavor in which we are involved, and we need spiritual tools to walk out the Christian life. Jesus said, "Apart from me you can do nothing" (John 15:5). Do you see that word, *nothing*? Jesus, by sending the Holy Spirit to indwell us, works his abiding work and brings forth fruit.

2. When we plug in to his power our batteries don't go dead. He is the "Ever-Ready" one. I believe that when Jesus said to take his yoke upon ourselves, he was saying that when we do his call in the power he has made available to us, the load will be lighter.

3. He will get the credit when what we do comes from his power. We can do a lot of "good things" in our own power, and often we get recognition for doing those things. As Christians, however, we want to be about the business of doing "God things" so that he receives the recognition. Too often people are enamored with a pastor or program rather than with the power of God. As we allow the Holy Spirit to work, and his tools to be evident, the credit (glory) will go to God.

63

Fantastic Fruit

Not only does the Holy Spirit deliver to us wonderful power tools, he also produces fine fruit. Paul wrote that the fruit of the Spirit is *evident* in the life of the believer.

> **Galatians 5:22-25:** "But the fruit of the Spirit is love, joy, peace, patience, kindness, goodness, faithfulness, gentleness, self-control; against such things there is no law. Now those who belong to Christ Jesus have crucified the flesh with its passions and desires. If we live by the Spirit, let us also walk by the Spirit."

Does an apple tree have to strain to produce apples? No! It is natural, because it is an apple tree. The fruit of the Spirit is a natural by-product of the indwelling presence of God in your life. Sometimes an apple tree needs pruning, or fertilizing... or special attention to be more productive, but apple production is its natural inclination. You may need some pruning, a little nurturing... perhaps some special attention, but if you indeed belong to Christ, Paul says that the "Holy Spirit Fruit" will be evident in your life.

The fruit of the Spirit is not something you can produce. You cannot *strain* enough to produce genuine spiritual love, joy, peace, and so forth. You may achieve some success at each of these on your own, but you can never experience them in fullest measure apart from Christ and the indwelling power of the Holy Spirit. Far too many Christians have tried to "muscle up" love, when what they really needed to do was surrender to the Holy Spirit, that he might create his fruit of love in the human heart.

What fruit do you see in your life as you walk by the Spirit?

Who's In Charge?

Every believer who has received Christ as Savior and Lord has received the gift of the Holy Spirit (Acts 2:38). It is evident, however, that some Christians seem to walk "according to the Spirit" more consistently than others. Some seem to experience greater power, greater fruit, and greater results as the Holy Spirit operates in and through them. Did God give more Holy Spirit to some than he did to others?

God gives gifts differently according to his will and purposes (1 Corinthians 12:11). Because of the variation in giftings, we will see God's power manifested differently in each other. We will not see, however, some Christians having more Holy Spirit than others. There are two key ingredients that foster the full manifestation of God's power in our lives.

1. Surrender

The more we give up to God, the more God gives to us to be all that he designed us to be. Paul said it well in Galatians 2:20:

> **Galatians 2:20:** "I have been crucified with Christ; and it is no longer I who live, but Christ lives in me; and the life which I now live in the flesh I live by faith in the Son of God, who loved me, and delivered himself up for me."

As we surrender and die to self, the more Christ's power is demonstrated in us. We put limitations on God by saying...

I'll do anything *but*...

or

I want all that you have for me *but*...

or

God, change any area of my life *but*...!

Our failure to surrender quenches the Spirit in our life. We resist him as did the stiffnecked religious leaders who stoned Stephen (Acts 7). The Holy Spirit is in us if we have indeed received Christ into our heart, but perhaps we have not fully surrendered to him.

* * *

Pause right now... ask God to help you search your heart to see if there is any area where you lack surrender to the leading of the Holy Spirit. Let go and let God have his way... and watch what happens!

* * *

2. Submission

Submission is day-to-day surrender. At the end of the Civil War, the Confederate troops surrendered. They were declaring their commitment to no longer fight or resist. Submitting to the authority of the Union Army, and ultimately reuniting as one nation, was a *process* of submission.

We may have willed in our hearts to surrender to all that God wants to do in and through us by the power of the Holy Spirit, but there is a daily submission process that must continue for us to fully realize his power. The Holy Spirit will lead, prompt, and encourage on a regular basis, and we must choose on a regular basis to submit.

In Conclusion

John 3:3-5: "Jesus answered and said to him, 'Truly, truly I say to you, unless one is born again, he cannot see the kingdom of God.' Nicodemus said to him, 'How can a man be born when he is old? He cannot enter a second time into his mother's womb and be born, can he?' Jesus answered, 'Truly, truly, I say to you, unless one is born of water and the Spirit, he cannot enter the kingdom of God.'"

Nicodemus was a good man. He was a very religious man. Jesus clearly said to him that he lacked the fresh, new birth of the Holy Spirit. We must be filled with the Holy Spirit. We can only bear fruit as we submit to the power of God to be manifested through us.

When God sends the Holy Spirit, he comes with gifts to empower us and produces eternal fruit to reflect his nature. Be filled with the Holy Spirit (Ephesians 5:18)!

Walking This Out...

Paul told the Galatians... and us... to walk in step with the Spirit. How do we do that?

Because the Holy Spirit is a person, I do everything I can to maintain a good relationship with him. I don't resist him when he directs. I don't quench him when he wants to work through me... and I don't intentionally grieve him, walking in rebellion. (At least, that is my heart's desire.)

That means I listen through the scriptures, others, circumstances, and his gentle nudges so I can be transformed by him. That means getting quiet enough to hear and being able to recognize his voice.

I remain open to his equipping gifts to accomplish his supernatural works through me.

I weed the garden of my heart, tilling the soil, watering the seed so that his good fruit will flourish.

Man of God! Walk in the Spirit!

Next Session

We will discuss the church in our next session. What is the nature of the church? Why do we have so many denominations? Why do we have "church fights"? Where do I fit in in the Body of Christ? Jesus loves his church! We are called his bride! It is important that we understand what is the purpose and design of his church.

Session 6

This Body The Church

(Where do I fit in?)

All Of These Body Parts

1 Corinthians 12:12-27: "For even as the body is one and yet has many members, and all the members of the body, though they are many, are one body, so also is Christ. For by one Spirit we were all baptized into one body, whether Jews or Greeks, whether slaves or free, and we were all made to drink of one Spirit. For the body is not one member, but many. If the foot should say, 'Because I am not a hand, I am not a part of the body,' it is not for this reason any less a part of the body. And if the ear should say, 'Because I am not an eye, I am not a part of the body,' it is not for this reason any the less a part of the body. If the whole body were an eye, where would the hearing be? If the whole were hearing, where would the sense of smell be? But now God has placed the members, each one of them, in the body, just as he desired. And if they were all one member, where would the body be? But now there are many members, but one body. And the eye cannot say to the hand, 'I have no need of you,' or again the head to the feet, 'I have no need of you.' On the contrary, it is much truer that the members of the body, which seem to be weaker, are necessary; and those members of the body, which we deem less honorable, on these we bestow more abundant honor, and our unseemly members come to have more abundant seemliness, whereas our seemly members have no need of it. But God has so composed the body, giving more abundant honor to that member which lacked, that there should be no division in the body, but that the members should have the same care for one another. And if one member suffers, all the members suffer with it; if one member is honored, all the members rejoice with it. Now you are Christ's body, and individually members of it."

Perhaps no other passage of scripture more clearly depicts how the church, the Body of Christ, ought to function than these verses. Paul, like Jesus, was a master at taking common, simple pictures to illustrate complex, spiritual truths. The imagery of a physical body presents a vivid allegory of Christ's body, the church. So what do these verses tell us about the church?

1. Every part has a part!

Because the foot is not a hand does not mean it is not a part. Because you might not sing in the choir or work in the nursery does not mean you don't have a part in the Body of Christ. If Jesus is in you, he has gifted you and given you purpose for his kingdom. Perhaps you have not discovered what that part is yet, but let me assure you, you are a vital part of Christ's body. One man told me that he thought he was the "pain in the neck." He really wasn't. He was more like the "funny bone." We are all needed in this beautiful Body of Christ. Discover your role and be faithful to walk in it.

2. The parts need each other!

The eye cannot say to the hand, "I have no need of you." Arrogance and independence do little to further the purposes of God. We should not think more highly of ourselves than we ought (Romans 12:3). We are all vitally important, but none of us is more important than another. In fact, we cannot function properly apart from one another.

* * *

I broke my "pinkie" on my left hand years ago and had to be put into a full cast from the elbow down. I didn't think much about it. It was only my pinkie — and it was my left hand. (I am right handed.) Boy,

72

was I in for a lesson. I could not drive my stick-shift Volkswagen! I couldn't even zip up my pants! But it was only my pinkie! I survived that ordeal, but I received firsthand a vivid picture of how all the body parts matter.

* * *

In the church today there is an independent attitude that borders on rebellion. For some, it is an attitude of "Jesus and me, that's all I need!" Paul clearly taught that we need each other in order to be effective for Christ. We are all different, with diverse giftings and passions, creating a beautiful necessary complement!

3. There cannot be division in the body!

What if my right leg chose to go right and my left leg chose to go left? Ouch! We all know that a divided house cannot stand. While we are beautifully diverse, we must be one in vision and purpose. On this road of faith, you may choose to travel in a Ford, Chevrolet, or Honda ... but we have to be traveling to the same destination with solid agreement on fundamentals of the faith.

A man said to me once that it really does not matter what you believe, as long as you believe something. One person told me that what really matters is sincerity, not necessarily truth. So... if I sincerely believe that eating strawberries every day will get me to heaven, then I am okay! (I'll call my church the "Shortcake Short-Cut Church.")

Contrary to much of what contemporary thought promotes, *there is such a thing as truth*! There are fundamentals of the faith that are essential to the unity of the church. The critical issue of our day is discerning clearly what those fundamentals are.

What beliefs do you consider to be fundamental to Christianity?

4. The body parts care for and about each other.

When one part weeps, we all do. When one part rejoices, we all do. That is a key ingredient to true "body life." When I hit my thumb with a hammer, my whole body gets involved. (Unfortunately my mouth takes an entirely too active role!) When we are connected by the blood of Christ as one, we care about each other. We empathize and participate in each other's pain and joy.

Because we care about each other, we do not go around wounding each other. If I continually hit myself over the head with a club, you would think that odd. Ultimately, I would probably be put under psychiatric observation and perhaps even treatment. People who injure themselves are not considered healthy. Body parts in the Body of Christ who injure other body parts are not healthy. When we deliberately attack or hurt others in the church, we have lost sight of the spiritual reality that we are connected.

Have you ever wounded someone or been wounded by someone in the Body of Christ?

5. Christ is the head of this body.

> **Ephesians 4:14-16:** "As a result, we are no longer to be children, tossed here and there by waves, and carried about by every wind of doctrine, by the trickery of men, by craftiness in deceitful scheming; but speaking the truth in love, we are to grow up in all aspects into him, who is the head, even Christ, from whom the whole body, being fitted and held together by that which every joint supplies, according to the proper working of each individual part, causes the growth of the body for the building up of itself in love."

We will experience great joy as well as powerful productivity as long as we submit to the headship of Christ over his church. When selfish ambition creeps in, or pride, or self-reliance, we will fall short of being the body he has called us to be. He is the head! **He is**

74

Lord! He is building his church and will enable us to be all that he has purposed us to be. It is essential that we submit to him.

* * *

I grew up on a farm in Missouri. We raised chickens. When a hen would stop laying eggs, it often became the main course at a Sunday lunch. We butchered our own hens, which always proved to be exciting. My mother would lay the broom handle across the neck of the hen and pull off the head, then release the bird. That headless chicken would run wildly around the yard for several minutes. It was dead and didn't know it. The dogs would bark madly. My four brothers and I would laugh and squeal. What a scene!

* * *

I think that is how it is in the church sometimes. We have lots of activity. There is plenty of noise — even excitement. But is it possible that that which has an appearance of "life" is actually "death" with headless misdirection?

We are not just a body. We are *the* Body of Christ... and he is the head!

What does it mean to you that Christ is the head of the church?

**If we're all one body...
then why are there so many churches?**

Division: The Source and Solution

1 Corinthians 11:18-19: "For, in the first place, when you come together as a church, I hear that divisions exist among you; and in part, I believe it. For there must also be factions among you in order that those who are approved may have become evident among you."

It must be absolutely clear that division in the Body of Christ is *never* God's best for us. Paul's words to the Corinthians about factions were more words of resignation rather than recommendation. Factions reveal those who truly belong to Christ (those who are approved). While the church of Corinth experienced great power and growth, it also was full of strife, immorality, and division. Paul is saying that the source of division was either carnal Christians or unbelievers in their midst.

When people make spiritual decisions void of spiritual guidance, there will be division and strife. Throughout the centuries the church has been plagued with people who put selfish desires ahead of the spiritual counsel of the Holy Spirit.

James addressed this same issue of division and strife with a similar conclusion:

> **James 3:14—4:1:** "But if you have bitter jealousy and selfish ambition in your heart, do not be arrogant and so lie against the truth. This wisdom is not that which comes from above, but is earthly, natural, demonic. For where jealousy and selfish ambition exist, there is disorder and every evil thing. But the wisdom from above is first, pure, then peaceable, gentle, reasonable, full of mercy and good fruits, unwavering, without hypocrisy. And the seed whose fruit is righteousness is sown in peace by those who make peace. What is the source of quarrels and conflicts among you? Is not the source your pleasures that wage war in your members?"

There is a war of the flesh going on in every one of us. We all struggle with jealousy and selfish ambition to some degree. When we give in to selfish desires, it often leads to strife and even division in the church.

Many church fights have little to do with theological issues. Often arguments ensue over carpet color, church building programs, pastoral selection, or other preference issues. Selfishness is often at the core of the inability to reconcile and work together as one. The reality is that there is still enough "sin" hanging around in the church that the goal of unity is difficult to achieve.

There have been occasions, however, in which theological issues were at stake. Because of significant differences of biblical interpretation or understandings of truth, some have considered it essential to no longer fellowship with certain individuals or groups. There are theological truths foundational to Christianity. To compromise those truths would be a participation in something less than Christian. For example, if you were connected with a church group that determined that Jesus was not the only begotten Son of God, but merely one among the great prophets, it would be difficult and even unwise to remain in fellowship with that group. It calls for real "spiritual wisdom" to discern which issues warrant separation.

Division Is Not Always Division

Just because we bear various denominational titles does not necessarily mean we are divided. Some of my richest fellowship and greatest experiences of unity have been with pastors of different denominations. The word denominate merely means "to name." It is not necessarily divisive to be "named" according to different distinctions as fellow Christians. Most denominational names are just that — a title reflecting a distinction of that fellowship.

Once I heard Jack Hayford speak about denominations. He likened them to tribes, like the tribes of Israel. The twelve tribes of Israel had their own name, flag, distinctions, but all knew they were one people: God's people! In the church of Jesus Christ there are many tribes, bearing many names, various "flags," and marked distinctions, but we are all purchased by the same blood, in submission to one Lord, destined for the same heaven.

There were times the tribes of Israel got prideful or argumentative, just as the tribes in the Body of Christ do today. God always brought Israel around when they got out of line, and I am confident that he will bring his bride, the church, into a place of full unity. Jesus prayed that we would be one... and one day we will.

Where Do I Fit In?

You are a part and have a part in the Body of Christ. Do you know how God has gifted you and what ministry in which you are to be involved? Our productivity in the kingdom of God is contingent upon our understanding of our purpose and empowerment. The man who does not know what he is to do or how he is to do it will not do much. Try these steps to discern your purpose and resources.

1. Fast and pray — seeking to know the Father's will.

Fasting is a way to be attentive to God.

> **Daniel 9:3:** "So I gave my attention to the Lord God to seek him by prayer and supplications with fasting, sackcloth, and ashes."

We discern better when we have an undistracted focus to hear the Lord. I have never made an important decision in my life without first fasting and praying. Every time I have fasted I have received the counsel of God.

The Bible has much to say about fasting. Here are a few biblical guidelines to fasting.

1. Fasting is a private activity. In fact, scripture discourages us from letting others know we are fasting. Privacy helps us avoid pridefulness (Matthew 6:16-18).

2. Fasting should be genuine, not mere religious activity. Sincerity is essential. Even wicked Jezebel fasted, but not genuinely (1 Kings 21:9-12).

3. Fast with a humble, unselfish heart. Be sure you are genuinely seeking the will of God (Zechariah 7:5).

4. A true fast needs to be significantly sacrificial. Jesus neither ate nor drank for forty days (Matthew 4:2). I do not recommend a fast of that intensity, but it does need to be significant to get to a place of attentiveness.

Fasting is clearly a means to get ourselves in a place to hear God better. If we truly want to know our part in the Body of Christ, we must earnestly seek him.

2. Seek godly counsel.

Talk to your pastor or another mature Christian to aid you in discerning what God is calling you to do or be as a part of the Body of Christ. What spiritual gifts have been imparted to you? Ask someone to help you discern that.

I strongly recommend that you participate in a spiritual gifts inventory. A good instrument for that is *Finding Your Spiritual Gifts*, Wagner-Modified Houts Questionnaire. Follow the instructions carefully as you complete the inventory. Meet with your pastor or a Christian advisor who knows you well to discern the results of the inventory.

3. Take some faith steps.

Moses did not really know he was the man for the job to lead Israel out of Egypt until he was in the middle of it. You may not know for sure what God is calling you to until you actually take steps to walk in it. Be willing to step out.

Where do you sense God may be calling you to get involved?

In Conclusion

We have really only scratched the surface when it comes to under-standing the church. The key to remember is that you are a part, and have a part, in this great fellowship of believers called the Body of Christ.

Walking This Out...

The church is not an organization, it is a living organism. It is made up of imperfect people who are on the journey together to know Jesus and to follow him. Battles have been fought, people have been hurt and disappointed... and the Spirit of God has been grieved by our unwillingness to submit to Jesus as head.

All that said, I love the church. It is the place to practice authentic love and walk in transparency before God and one another. It is a place to find healing, hope, and help in our time of need. It is a beautiful body, the bride of Christ, being made more radiant by our groom.

As part of the church, I ask not what I can get, but what I can give. I come not to get fed, but to feed. I do not come to be heard, but to hear... not to be understood, but to understand. Looking to love, to forgive, to reconcile rather than to find those for myself, I find being a part of Christ's church very fulfilling.

Men, don't wait to be asked to serve! Serve! Body part... do your part!

Next Session

Jesus said that when we worship we should do so in spirit and in truth (John 4:24). What is true, spiritual worship? Why is worship an important part of our Christian pilgrimage? Worship is our topic in the next session.

Session 7

Spiritual Worship

(What is worship... and why?)

True Spiritual Worship

1 Chronicles 16:29: "Give unto the Lord the glory due his name; bring an offering, and come before him; worship the Lord in the beauty of holiness."

John 4:23-24: "But an hour is coming, and now is, when the true worshipers shall worship the Father in Spirit and truth, for such people the Father seeks to be his worshipers. God is Spirit, and those who worship him must worship in Spirit and truth."

A man will never be all he is to be until he grasps who God is. The wisest man who ever lived wrote, "The fear of the Lord is the beginning of wisdom" (Proverbs 9:10). We "wise up" when we have a reverence for God. When we comprehend how awesome, holy, majestic, powerful, just, and loving God is, wisdom reveals to us our own finitude. Both our beginning and our end are found in God. Apart from him, life holds no hope or purpose. Solomon also wrote, "The fear of the Lord is a fountain of life" (Proverbs 14:27). As we grow in our reverence (fear), adoration, and worship of God, we receive the impartation of wisdom and life.

Worship is key to maintaining a heart of reverence and adoration before God. Jesus said the Father is looking for true worshipers. We must worship him in Spirit and in truth. Because worship is so vital to our Christian walk... so central to our Christian life... it is crucial for us to understand what true spiritual worship is. How do we live out a life of spiritual worship? Why is worship so important?

What Is Worship?

Worship is an expression of adoration or reverence for God. It is both an attitude and an activity. It is an event, and it is also a lifestyle. In the Bible three different words are used for worship. While all three are translated to worship, they each carry distinctive meaning.

Proskuneo (literally, to kiss the hand)

This Greek word, translated to worship, is a picture of respect, dignity, and intimacy. Worship is an expression of emotion and devotion to one held in highest esteem.

Shahah (literally, to bow down)

This is a Hebrew word. The picture is one of homage, as before a master or king. While God is loving Father, he is also reigning Lord and king. Worship remembers that!

Therapeuo (literally, to serve)

This Greek word sounds a bit like therapy, doesn't it? Actually, our word "therapy" comes from *therapeuo*. While the word literally means "to serve," it is translated as both worship and service in the scriptures. Worship is a life of joyous service to God. Paul alluded to this aspect of worship when he wrote to the Christians at Rome:

> **Romans 12:1:** "Present your bodies as a living and holy sacrifice, acceptable to God, which is your spiritual service of worship."

Worship is a lifestyle of daily submission to honor God. Worship involves all that we are and all that we do. It is an attitude of the heart that seeks to adore and honor God in all things.

In Spirit

Worship apart from the Spirit is religious ritual or routine. The Spirit leads us into a place of true spiritual worship by revealing to us who God is (John 16:13-15), and who we are as sons (Romans 8:16). Having the Spirit of God in our lives makes us heirs to the kingdom of God. Jesus told Nicodemus, "Truly, I say to you, unless one is born of water and the Spirit, he cannot enter into the kingdom of God" (John 3:5). As partakers of God's kingdom, by revelation and empowerment of the Holy Spirit, we offer up true spiritual worship. As those who experience God's kingdom of righteousness, peace, and joy in the Holy Spirit (Romans 14:17), true spiritual worship emerges from our lives.

In Truth

There must be a sincerity about our worship. We cannot fool God with our phoniness. Let's take a look at what the prophet Isaiah wrote was going on in the hearts of the people of Israel.

> **Isaiah 29:13:** "Then the Lord said, 'Because this people draw near with their words and honor me with their lip service, but they remove their hearts far from me, and their reverence for me consists of tradition learned by rote.' "

True worship is from the heart. It is not just going through the motions. It is both attitude and activity flowing from genuine adoration for God.

Worship in Spirit and in truth are really "heart" issues. Is the heart surrendered to and filled with the Spirit of God? Is the heart genuinely set on honoring and blessing God? The heart is at the crux of worship, exceeding the importance of any actions or activities we may be involved in that are considered worship. You can be religious, doing a lot of religious activities, but if there is a heart problem, it is not true spiritual worship.

Is your worship authentic?

Worship In Action

While heart attitude is central to true worship, there are certain actions or activities that typically flow from a heart set on honoring God.

SERVICE:

A life of service will mark a true worshiper. There is an attitude of gratitude for who God is and all that he has done that spurs us to lay our lives down for him. Paul wrote in Philippians, "For me to live is Christ" (Philippians 1:21). Because Christ had given Paul life, hope, and purpose, his whole life was set on honoring Christ. Someone once said that *life is a gift from God. What we do with it is our gift back to him.* A life given back to him in honorable service is worship.

PHYSICAL EXPRESSIONS:

Worship is expressed with various activities. Often our scripture worship is full of physical participation. We see movement. We hear sounds and songs. Worship is more than an attitude. It is a response that is expressed in many and various ways that involve the totality of our being. Let's take a look at a list of just a few biblical expressions of worship.

Biblical Expressions Of Worship

SINGING: "O come, let us sing for joy to the Lord" (Psalm 95:1).
DANCING: "Let them praise his name with dancing!" (Psalm 149:3).
SHOUTING: "Let us shout joyfully to the rock of our salvation" (Psalm 95:1).
RAISING HANDS: "Hear the voice of my supplications when I cry to thee for help, when I lift up my hands toward thy holy sanctuary" (Psalm 28:2).
CLAPPING: "O clap your hands, all people!" (Psalm 47:1).

INSTRUMENTS: "Raise a song, strike the timbrel, the sweet sounding lyre with the harp" (Psalm 81:2).

BOWING OR KNEELING: "Come let us worship and bow down; let us kneel before the Lord our maker" (Psalm 95:6).

SILENCE: "There will be silence before thee, and praise in Zion, O God" (Psalm 65:1).

Of the biblical expressions of worship, which have you experienced or expressed?

singing	instruments
dancing	bowing
shouting	kneeling
raising hands	silence
clapping	other

Why Is Worship So Important?

Worship Honors God:

> **Psalm 108:3-5:** "I will give thanks to thee, O Lord, among the peoples; and I will sing praises to thee among the nations. For thy loving kindness is great above the heavens; and thy truth reaches to the skies. Be exalted, O God, above the heavens, and thy glory above all the earth."

God is so great! What a wonderful loving Father! What a just and powerful king! He is a faithful, caring friend! It is a joy to bless and honor him.

You see, God is not some abstract concept. He is a person. He created us in his image and he pursues fellowship with us.

> **John 3:16:** "For God so loved the world, that he gave his only begotten Son, that whoever believes in him should not perish, but have eternal life."

It was his love for us that prompted him to sacrifice his Son. It was not so that we would serve him. He was pursuing a love relationship with us. Worship is our expression of love back to God. Worship deepens and expands that wonderful love relationship with him! It blesses and honors him!

* * *

> My son, Ben, came up to me one time and said, "Dad, you're the greatest!" He proceeded to give me a huge hug and kiss. My eyes welled up with tears, my heart pounded with emotion as I returned hugs and kisses to my son. He had blessed and honored his father and our relationship deepened. God loves to hear his children express their love. He delights in the praises of his people. It honors and blesses him.

* * *

Worship Changes Us:

Worship keeps our perspective of how limited we are and how limitless he is! Worship quiets our anxious hearts as we remember that our powerful, loving king is securely on his throne, caring for us. When we focus on the holiness of God, our sin becomes more apparent and the Spirit of God prompts us to repent. When we sense his love for us as we express our love to him, our love for others grows. Worship changes us in so many ways.

How have you been changed during a time of expressing worship?

In Conclusion

Your heart committed to Christ is the key to true spiritual worship. This may be a real growth area for you. Be encouraged. The nature of relationships is growth, including our relationship with the Lord of the universe. As that relationship grows, so shall your heart to worship in Spirit and in truth.

Walking This Out...

For me, worship is like a divine romance. Just like with my wife, there are times that are more intimate, more intense than others, but every moment of our relationship is an expression of covenant love even in what seems like mundane everyday activity.

That means I look for God in the everyday stuff. I listen for his voice in the expression of intimate worship songs... or listening to '70s music with my daughter. I desire to please him, to honor him, to love him moment by moment every day. I find what makes that happen is dependent upon how I start the day. My quiet time serves as a rudder for the day in worship.

Recently on a radio talk show I heard a guy ask, "How many of you give your spouse a peck in the morning as you go your separate ways?" He suggested, "Try a seven-second kiss and I guarantee your day will be different." Amazing! I find myself thinking about my wife all day.

Men, kiss the face of God as you begin your day and you will walk in a life of worship!

Next Session

Men! We are encouraged in scripture to be men! (1 Corinthians 13:16). We are to be godly husbands and fathers. What is our biblical role as head of our home? How can we fulfill that role more effectively? Let's dig in and be men... faithful men of God.

Session 8

Spiritual Husbandry

(Loving as Jesus loves)

Being A Godly Man

1 Corinthians 16:13: "Be on the alert, stand firm in the faith, act like men. Be strong."

We have a tremendous responsibility as men of God to be faithful to our call. We are to be alert, stand firm in the faith, and be strong. That admonition is true whether we are a single man, a husband, or a dad. By God's grace and with the empowerment of the Holy Spirit, we can walk in faithfulness and integrity to the challenge set before us. Let's be godly men.

Before you flex your "spiritual muscles," let me give you a couple of words of encouragement. First of all, God will provide you with what you need to fulfill the responsibility as a husband. Philippians 4:13 says, "I can do all things through Christ who strengthens me." Success begins with surrender to his Holy Spirit working through you.

Secondly, you must take initiative to grow and become all that you can be. The mark of a great teacher is that he continues to be a student himself. As I learn about being a husband, I learn that I need to learn more. Be teachable. Pursue wisdom, knowledge, and skill. Let God grow you into your full potential as a husband.

Where a man "is" in his spiritual growth does not matter nearly as much as where he is headed!

Spiritual Husbandry

Let's take a look at some biblical principles prompting us to be godly husbands. What a delight... what a responsibility to take a woman as your wife. When my bride walked that aisle on our wedding day my heart pounded with both joy and holy fear. (I think it was holy.) I had only a small idea of the role God was calling me to as the husband of that beautiful bride. Marriage is one of the most important God-ordained institutions on the planet. He takes those vows we make very seriously, and so should we.

Here Comes The Groom

Jeff Crabtree, a dear pastor friend, was serving as featured speaker at a conference I attended. He opened his remarks with these words, "Have you ever wondered why the man is called the bridegroom, but the woman is not called the groom bride?" He certainly stimulated my thoughts with that statement.

Men, we have a grooming responsibility unto our wives that they do not need to reciprocate. I must admit, I immediately thought of our horse we had on the small farm in Missouri when I was a boy. I groomed her regularly. While there are some parallels to what went on at our Missouri home, being a groom to your bride is not "horsing" around.

Grooming Tips: How To Nurture A Beautiful Wife

1. Praise her. We do not compliment our wives enough. Be specific in your praise. Do it sincerely and do it often. For many women, their husbands are their primary feedback source. Give her genuine praise and watch her glow!

2. Listen to her. One of the best ways to express genuine love and care for her well-being is to listen to her. When you come home, make it a point to ask her how her day was... and when you ask, be attentive to her response.

3. Express affection apart from sexual advances. Often in counseling I hear the wife complain that the only time her husband expresses affection is when he wants sex. Is your wife suspicious when you give her a squeeze or meet her with a kiss that you've got one eye on her and one eye on the bedroom? It is too easy to allow our wives to become the object of our sexual gratification rather than the recipient of our genuine, devoted affection.

4. Say thank you! Don't just grunt and belch as gratitude for a great meal. Say thank you! Do you see all that clean laundry put away neatly in your drawer? Do not take that for granted. Be an appreciative husband for the woman God gave to you.

5. Do not forget your anniversary. Birthdays and other special days may not mean as much to you, but they usually are very important to your wife. It grooms her well to affirm her preciousness by remembering those special occasions.

6. Carry the largest load. If you want to wear your wife out and break her down, let her carry the bulk of the responsibility in the home. God's word calls the woman the weaker vessel. That does not mean she is of any lesser value, but like fine china, she needs greater care. Too many women carry too much, if not most, of the load when it comes to the management of the home.

7. Give her time for refreshment. Encourage her to get away for a day or two to rest and have quiet time with God. Support her in participating in a Christian women's group so that she will have a source of refreshment from friends.

8. Remember her on the ordinary days. It is one thing to send a card or flowers on a special day. How about taking her out in the middle of the week just so the two of you can have some time together? Or send those flowers on a Monday just because she is the woman you love!

9. Never demean her. Too often I hear men call their bride their "old lady" in public, often in her presence. Painful criticisms become public domain for insensitive husbands. Never demean your wife, publicly or privately.

10. Be a one-woman man. Do not look to the left or to the right. Assure your wife that she truly is your one and only. Don't compare her to other women. If you are accustomed to teasing with your wife about other women, resolve to stop now! One-woman devotion is a serious matter to your wife.

How are you doing as a bridegroom?

Be A House-Band

I remember as a young man hearing a pastor speak of the meaning of the word husband. He said that the word husband came from the combination of two words: house and band. A husband has a role as protector or guardian of his wife. There is to be a place of security for her in his care. Perhaps the encouragement found in 1 Corinthians 16 has its greatest application in this role as husband.

> "Be on the alert, stand firm in the faith, act like men. Be strong!"
> 1 Corinthians 16:13

BE ON THE ALERT:

There are so many forces coming against marital union. With more than half of marriages ending in divorce, we have ample evidence to see that keeping a strong, healthy marriage is no easy task. We must be alert to all that will come against our marriage and be prepared to respond to the attacks.

We must be especially attentive to the spiritual forces that we are up against. Paul reminded us in his letter to the Ephesians of the spiritual battle:

Ephesians 6:10-12: "Finally, be strong in the Lord, and in the strength of his might. Put on the full armor of God, that you may be able to stand firm against the schemes of the devil. For our struggle is not against flesh and blood, but against the rulers, against the powers, against the world forces of this darkness, against the spiritual forces of wickedness in the heavenly places."

Be alert, men! We cannot afford to put our heads in the sand and ignore the onslaught coming against our most important human relationship.

BE FIRM IN THE FAITH:

We must know what we believe and be biblically grounded in our faith. Too many men have relinquished the spiritual leadership in the home to their wives and have become content with mediocrity when it comes to their own biblical knowledge and understanding. In order to protect your wife and marriage from destructive false philosophies, you must be grounded in truth.

BE STRONG:

We are not talking about being "macho" when we talk about strength. We must be strong in the Lord. May it be said of you as it was said of Stephen, the first martyr of the Christian faith, "they chose Stephen, a man full of faith and of the Holy Spirit" (Acts 6:5). And again the scriptures say that he was a man "full of grace and power" (Acts 6:8). Stephen was a man of great strength, fully founded in God.

Let Your Helper Help

Genesis 2:18: "Then the Lord God said, 'It is not good for the man to be alone. I will make him a helper suitable for him.'"

The word *helper* used to describe Eve is the same word used of the

Holy Spirit (John 14:16) and even of God himself in Psalm 30:10. The wife has a vital role in this marital relationship. Learn to let her be your helper. It will benefit both of you.

Receive her encouragement. Just as the Holy Spirit is our "comforter," God gave your wife to you to encourage you. Listen to her. Receive those words of encouragement and comfort.

Receive her correction. The Holy Spirit as helper convicts of sin. Too often we dismiss the constructive criticism of our wives as nagging. The criticism you receive from your wife should receive the highest consideration.

Receive her counsel. Sometimes we don't like to hear our wives say, "Wait," when it comes to a business venture or large purchase. Experience has taught me that she usually is absolutely right. If your wife gives you counsel about other relationships, listen carefully to her words. I am not suggesting that we blindly accept the counsel of our wives; however, I would encourage you never to ignore it.

How well do you receive counsel from your wife?

Just Like Jesus

Ephesians 5:25: "Husbands, love your wives, just as Christ also loved the church and gave himself up for her."

How much did Jesus love the church? Enough to die for her? How much must a husband love his wife? Enough to *live* for her. We lay down our lives for our wives by sacrificially expressing our love and devotion to them. Most women are not interested in our dying for them. They are interested in seeing a daily, living expression of real love.

In my short years of marriage, I have discovered some areas of sacrificial love that are important to my wife.

Take time with her. Be willing to turn off the football game. Don't stay late at work so often. Put her ahead of your chores at home. Don't let a newspaper or book serve as a wall between you. Have plenty of quality time that affirms her significance in your life.

Respond promptly to her requests. How long has that faucet dripped? You will get to that broken door latch when? Putting off genuine needs of your wife sends her a message of neglect. Sacrificially serve to express your love.

Do your part around the home. I had one wife tell me that her children were ages 6, 11, 13, and 39. I got her point. She went on to express great frustration and hurt for having to pick up after her husband. She felt like a maid, not a bride. Lay down your life by picking up your socks.

Eat crow regularly. Why is saying, "I'm sorry," so hard? Why do we choke at the phrase, "I was wrong"? Humility works as a wonderful glue in a marriage. Do not be afraid to admit mistakes and to ask for forgiveness. Laying pride down is part of dying to self.

Keep on courting her. More than one woman has told me that the man she married was not the man who courted her. That wonderful man who sacrificially served, loved, and nurtured her became some monarch on a throne after the wedding vows. Always see her as precious and remind her often of her preciousness to you.

How do you express Christlike love to your wife?

Keep growing in your role as husband. Be willing to participate with your wife in marriage enrichment events. Read books with wise biblical counsel on the subjects of marriage. Every moment you invest will cause both you and your wife to reap great reward.

In Conclusion

Men, do not feel overwhelmed with the responsibilities of being a husband. Let me remind you that you can do it in the strength Christ gives you. We are all learning and growing. Just keep headed in the right direction allowing God to enable you to be all that he wants you to be.

Walking This Out...

Men, being a godly husband is one of our toughest assignments. After all, we are called to die to ourselves for our wives. No one ever said dying would be easy, especially with our egos.

That's why I need other men, especially older men to help me on this journey as a husband. It is so helpful to know you don't go it alone, and that other men have similar struggles. Often they bring Spirit-led solutions to those struggles.

I pursue walking in mutual submission to Christ when it comes to my marriage. When we have a conflict I go to the one who glued us together. Many times I have heard him say, "Daryl, you are so wrong on this one. Go make it right."

I resist the enemy of our marriage. God loves marriage since it reflects our relationship with him... and guys, look who we are in that picture. The devil knows if he can take you out, he has crushed the picture of God's covenant love. Tell that devil where to go!

Husbands... love your wives!

Next Session

It is a crucial role we are called to as spiritual head of the house. Not only are we encouraged to be godly husbands, but we must be godly dads. In our next session we will consider our responsibilities as fathers. One of the greatest investments in life is what you deposit in the hearts and lives of your children. We will also consider what it means to be a spiritual father, providing guidance to non-biological sons in the faith.

Session 9

Faithful Fathering

(Raising up
a spiritual heritage)

Faithful Fathering

We have a great responsibility as men to nurture those whom God has entrusted to our care. By both teaching and example we are to point our sons and daughters to Christ and godly principles (Deuteronomy 6:6-7). By God's grace and with the empowerment of the Holy Spirit we are enabled to be faithful fathers. Although we will fail from time to time we must press on to fulfill our responsibility. When you fail, don't quit! Just press in closer to the one who enables you. Ask his forgiveness (and that of your child or perhaps your wife) and begin again.

In this session we will consider several biblical principles relating to our role as dads. First we will consider the role of spiritual fathers, or mentors, then move on to the subject of biological or by-law fathers.

Spiritual Dads

Not all men are husbands or biological fathers. All men, however, have the opportunity to be spiritual fathers. The Apostle Paul is a good example of a single man who was a terrific spiritual dad. In our closing session the entire focus will be on men mentoring men (being a spiritual mentor or father in the faith), but it seems pertinent now at least to call attention to the role of spiritual fathers.

Let's consider five important ingredients to spiritual parenting. Just to make it a little easier to remember these five aspects, they are arranged in an acrostic that spells *PLATE*. Think of it as an opportunity to provide spiritual "nutrition" and growth for the one you are discipling.

P = PRAY

Commit to pray regularly for that man you have taken under your wing as a son. Ask him often for specific prayer concerns. Remember to check on the outcome of the prayers as you progress in your relationship.

Not only pray *for* your spiritual son, pray *with* him. I have met with many men in restaurants and never hesitated to pray with them. Don't think it strange to pray with him over the phone. Give him a call, especially if he is going through a difficult time, and pray right then over the phone.

L = LOVE

Love him genuinely with the love of Christ. Do not see him as a project or assignment, but as a person whom you sincerely care about. Be willing to be vulnerable and tenderhearted with him as with a son. I am convinced that Paul loved Timothy as a son, not as a student.

A = ACCOUNTABILITY

Accountability is essential to good growth. Do not be controlling, but be willing to be challenging. Often I have seen too much grace applied and growth is stifled. Do not let him off the hook when he really doesn't need to be.

T = TEACH

Teach him biblical truth. Don't just get together and talk about whatever is on your mind. Intentionally get into the word of God, even if only briefly at times. I will recommend mentoring resources in our final session.

E = EXEMPLIFY CHRIST

Reflect the nature and teaching of Jesus Christ before your spiritual son. Your actions and attitudes will speak more powerfully than your words. Paul had the confidence to say, "Be imitators of me, just as I also am of Christ" (1 Corinthians 11:1). Be an example.

These are good beginning steps to being a spiritual father in the faith. The best spiritual fathering flows from a real relationship of genuine love and concern.

Do you see a man to whom you can serve as a spiritual father?

Biological Or By-Law Dads

The role of spiritual dad or mentor is often an "elective" relationship. Being a biological father or stepfather is a predetermined relationship. We enter into it differently and live it out differently. According to scripture our responsibility is not elective either. It is predetermined by God.

> **Malachi 4:5-6:** "Behold, I am going to send you Elijah the prophet before the coming of the great and terrible day of the Lord. And he will restore the hearts of the fathers to their children, and the hearts of the children to their fathers, lest I come and smite the land with a curse."

We see in our day a deep need for the restoration of the father-child relationship. Nearly 40% of children today live in a home absent of a father. In far too many homes, while the father is present he is nearly a stranger to his children. He knows little of the interests, activities, and developments of his children. May God restore the hearts of the fathers to their children in this generation.

The Bible is clear as to our role and responsibilities as fathers. Let us be challenged to adhere to the biblical standard God has set before us. Resolve that you will diligently pursue being a godly father.

As we consider several biblical mandates regarding our role as fathers, be open to the areas the Holy Spirit might be growing you. God's calling is high, the responsibilities great, but God will enable you to be the dad he wants you to be.

Bringing Home The Bacon

Being a good provider for our family is an admonition of the Lord:

> **1 Timothy 5:8:** "If anyone does not provide for his own, and especially for those of his household, he has denied the faith and is worse than an unbeliever."

Those are strong words! Certainly at times there are extenuating circumstances when it comes to the role as provider. A layoff or injury cannot be foreseen. Paul's words to Timothy were in reference to a dad who failed to provide due to irresponsibility, laziness, or lack of diligence. We are called to do all within our power to be faithful providers.

When I was six years old my dad suffered a massive heart attack and nearly died. He was forced by his poor health to give up a good-paying job as a fireman. Our income level and standard of living experienced a radical shift. I still remember my uncle coming to my dad and encouraging him to get on government assistance. Dad chose to work odd jobs that were less stressful and provided for our family's needs. (I have four brothers.) To this day my heart is full of gratitude for my father's provision.

One of the areas in which it seems that God is bringing strong conviction today is in the area of child support. Too many dads have shirked their responsibility for their children because a divorce or separation has taken place. Those children are still their children! The obligation as a provider has not changed. Be faithful in your role as a father.

One word of caution: Please do not think that being provider means providing for all of the "wants" of your children. I have seen dads knocking themselves out working far too many hours under the false notion that they are responsible to meet all of the wants of their children. You serve your children better by providing their needs and instructing them in sound values when it comes to material possessions.

Doing Discipline Right!

> **Hebrews 12:7:** "It is for discipline that you endure; God deals with you as with sons; for what son is there whom his father does not discipline?"

> **Proverbs 19:18:** "Discipline your son while there is hope, and do not desire his death."

Discipline and punishment are not one and the same. Have you ever heard a parent say, "I had to discipline my child," when what they actually did was punish the child? The word "discipline" has a direct correlation with the word "disciple." A disciple is a learner or follower. To discipline your children is to train or instruct. Instruction may be accompanied by verbal or physical admonition at times; however, instruction does not always involve correction. Instruction is at the heart of discipline. Fathers are to be about the business of providing biblical moral instruction to their children.

What is your greatest weakness when it comes to disciplining your children?

Teaching The Truth

> **Deuteronomy 6:6-7:** "And these words, which I am commanding you today, shall be on your heart; and you shall teach them diligently to your sons and shall talk of them when you sit in your house and when you walk by the way and when you lie down and when you rise up."

How many dads leave it up to Mom, or to the Sunday school, or to Christian school to teach their children biblical truths? While teaching is not all on the shoulders of the father, it is an important part of his role. When the father is not doing the teaching directly, he is responsible to guard his children from error to ensure that they are receiving sound teaching.

Teaching your child Christian principles is not necessarily done in a classroom setting. The passage from Deuteronomy makes it clear that it is a daily, moment-by-moment activity accomplished in all aspects of life. Seize each "teaching moment" as it comes.

* * *

I took my children to the playground one afternoon, giving Mom a much deserved rest. We had not been there long when my son came up to me crying. He informed me that a "bully" was throwing sand in the faces of other children. After comforting Ben, I asked, "What do you think Jesus would do in this situation?" Ben said he wasn't sure how Jesus would handle this, although he knew Jesus would not throw sand back. We considered the options, discussing several biblical examples of Jesus in times of conflict. We prayed for the little boy, then I went over with Ben and asked the little boy to stop throwing sand. It was a great teaching opportunity and my son went away from that park that day with a greater grasp of the love and compassion God has for the sinner. He also saw the value of praying before you act in response to someone who has hurt or offended you. Seize those teaching moments.

* * *

Share a "teaching moment" you have experienced.

Do As I Say... And As I Do

Ephesians 4:1: "I, therefore, the prisoner of the Lord, entreat you to walk in a manner worthy of the calling with which you have been called."

Do you ever allow yourself to walk in a double standard before your children? It frustrates and confuses your children when they hear you say one thing and see you do another. The very thing we may chastise them for we turn around and do. Do you allow your children to get away with temper tantrums? Probably not. How often do they see you rant and rave with outbursts of anger? Is it okay for them to call a friend or sibling stupid? Certainly not! Do you remember that "stupid cop" that pulled you over on the way to the skating party? When your child promised to take out the trash and failed to get it done, did he receive a rebuke? Think of all of the promises you have broken, yet your "good excuses" dismiss any charges against you.

Integrity means we are what we say. We call ourselves to the same high biblical standard to which we call our children. Yes, we will make mistakes. When we do, we need to acknowledge them to our children, not make excuses. Do not be afraid to ask forgiveness of your child.

Tell about a time you found yourself correcting your child for something of which you were guilty.

Point To Jesus

During my years in ministry I have been amazed at the number of children who grew up in a Christian home who met Christ at a crusade, revival, or church camp. I commend the parents for having sown the seeds of righteousness and for setting a godly example before their children. What has caught my attention, however, is the number of Christian parents who either do not know how, or never think to introduce their own children to the person of Jesus Christ.

You may be a great provider. You may serve well as a disciplinarian, teacher, and example. If your children do not see that a personal relationship with Jesus Christ is at the heart of it all, you have failed to impart real life to them. Point your children to the person of Jesus Christ. Instruct them clearly in the necessity of his sacrificial love expressed on the cross. Jesus was not just a good teacher we follow. He is the very Son of God, the way, the truth, and the life. He is the only source for the forgiveness of sin and the gift of everlasting life. Let your children know those truths and let them see that Jesus lives in you.

Do your children know that Jesus is at the center of your life?

In Conclusion

It's exciting and challenging being a father. With the increase in the number of single dads and step-dads challenges today are even greater. With a culture that seldom affirms sound, biblical family values, we are swimming against an adverse tide. God's word and the power of the Holy Spirit are just as relevant and able to address those challenges. Be encouraged! Pursue the high standard to which God calls us. Be a faithful father: faithful to Christ... and faithful to your children.

Walking This Out...

I don't think there is a greater privilege or a greater responsibility than being a father. Being a father is the awareness that someone else is watching you... modeling their life after yours whether intentionally or accidentally.

It seems to me the most important ingredient to fathering is authenticity. Present authentic faith, love, actions, values, and character in such a way that honor the Lord Jesus Christ and you will do well. In other words, be real, and be the same man every day and everywhere.

Love your kids as your heavenly Father loves you. Nothing separates us from his love. Don't put up any walls that would fence your kids out from the reality of your love. Love them enough to pray for them every day.

My biological children are all out of the nest now and I'm learning even more about the adventure of fathering... and now grandfathering. Advice should be given to our adult children sparingly. In fact, I have told my married children that I will only give advice when asked. (Tongue biting is encouraged.) I have been encouraged and amazed to watch the two of them work through things together.

Be glad you are a dad!

Next Session

Our next session has a strong relationship to our last two sessions. We will be discussing integrity. We will consider integrity in the home and outside the home. In every aspect of life we are called to be men of integrity. Integrity is "moral soundness or purity; incorruptness; uprightness; honesty." God has called us to a high standard as godly men.

Session 10

The Real Thing

(The priority of integrity)

Integrity: The Real Thing

Integrity is moral soundness or purity; incorruptness; uprightness; honesty. The word "integrity" is also used to describe jewels or costly metals. Gold of high integrity is very pure. Diamonds without flaws, chips, or cracks are considered to be of the highest degree of integrity.

How pure is your life? Are there moral flaws that hinder you from being all that God wants you to be? Are there cracks that diminish your radiance as a servant of God? I have good news. God has a solution for all those flaws and will refine you to shine in his glory. He is in the business of dealing with impurities — that's what the cross is all about! He is changing us by the power of the Holy Spirit, transforming us to be more like him.

We do have a part, however, in this matter of integrity. We must surrender our all to him to let him accomplish his full purposes in us. Too often there are areas of our life that we cling to that we know do not please him, yet we resist surrender to his will.

* * *

It didn't seem like a big deal to me. It was something I had always done. I used the phrase, "A lot of people," a lot of the time. "A lot of people think we ought to build a new building." "A lot of people think the choir sings too many old songs." It might have been true. I was pretty sure it was true. But the Holy Spirit nudged me and said, "Do you know it to be true that a lot of people feel this way... or that way?"

I kept using the phrase. A lot of people, after all, like to have you back up your opinion with the phrase "a lot of people." Finally the Lord spoke succinctly and said, "You are a liar!" That got my attention and I saw just how hideous my presumptuous exaggeration was. I surrendered my deceptive tongue to the Lord and he has done a refining work.

* * *

Not only must we surrender to let God work in every area of our lives, but we must diligently exercise self-control, persevering to a place of victory. I have met men who seemed to want God to sprinkle some "magic dust" on them that would remove the moral flaw with which they struggled.

God does supernaturally deliver us from many sinful struggles, but there are also times we must resolve in our hearts to exercise diligent self-control. I heard a man say once, "If God really wants me to quit smoking then he will make cigarettes taste bad to me." He might do that. He might say, "Stop buying the cigarettes!" One young man found freedom and deliverance from an addiction to pornography by resolving in his heart not to enter into establishments that sold pornography. It was no easy, wave-of-the-hand fix. It was a diligent pursuit of moral excellence which God met with his grace to enable this young man to overcome! In the final pages of this session we will consider a few beginning steps to overcoming immorality or impurity.

Is there an area of moral flaw in which you lack diligent self-control and perseverance? Can you name those areas so others can pray for you?

Integrity Is A Heart Issue

Matthew 5:8: "Blessed are the pure in heart for they shall see God."

Proverbs 4:23: "Watch over your heart with all diligence, for from it flow the springs of life."

Psalm 139:23-24: "Search me, O God, and know my heart; Try me and know my anxious thoughts; and see if there be any hurtful way in me, and lead me in the everlasting way."

Psalm 51:10: "Create in me a clean heart, O God, and renew a steadfast spirit within me."

David was a great and godly king. Just casual reading of the psalms reveals how much David loved God. God worked mightily in his life. Even with his great devotion, David had moral flaws. In fact, he was guilty of both murder and adultery. After David committed adultery with Bathsheba and organized the death of her husband, he knew what his real problem was. He had a heart problem. Rather than muscle up and say, "I'll not do that again!" or make pledges to "do better next time," he cried out to God, "Create in me a clean heart." He knew the place to get back on track to walk in integrity was in his heart.

When I think of the heart I think of emotions. As men, we cannot let our emotions dictate our integrity. The slogan, "If it feels right, do it," does not work! The heart is deceitful; therefore, we must be on guard and often ask God to search our hearts and reveal those "wicked ways" in us.

Matters of the heart are related to our mind. Notice how many of the verses that speak to the heart speak also to the mind. Men, we must be careful what we take into our thoughts, and where we let our thoughts wander. We are to "take every thought captive to the obedience of Christ" (2 Corinthians 10:5). Don't fill your mind with thoughts and opinions that are contrary to the example and commands of Christ Jesus.

Secret Sins Nurtured
In The Heart And In The Mind

When is a thought or attitude sin? Is a casual glance at the opposite sex sin? If one's eyes remained fixed for more than ten seconds on the pornography section in the convenience store, does that constitute sin? As that shiny new car zips by and you think to yourself, "I'd sure like one of those," have you coveted?

Unger's Bible Dictionary helps us understand when we have crossed the line into sinful thoughts or desires:

Lust: "In the ethical sense lust is used to express sinful desire — sinful either in being directed toward forbidden objects, or in being violent as to overcome self-control, and to engross the mind with earthly, carnal, and perishable things."

Covetousness: "An inordinate desire for what one has not, which has its basis in discontentment with what one has. It has an element of lawlessness, and is sinful because contrary to the command, 'Be content with such things as ye have' " (Hebrews 13:5).

While these definitions are helpful, it is still difficult to discern when we have crossed the line and wandered into sin in our secret thoughts and desires. That is why it is so important to ask God to search your heart and mind and to reveal sin to you. He is faithful and by his Holy Spirit will bring conviction. Be attentive to hear and be willing to respond appropriately.

When do you think a thought has "crossed the line" and has become a sinful lust?

Secret Sins Behind Closed Doors

The measure of a man is who he is in secret. In other words, the true test of moral integrity is discovered when no one is watching.

John 3:19-20: "And this is the judgment, that the light is come into the world, and men loved the darkness rather than the light; for their deeds were evil. For everyone who does evil hates the light, and does not come to the light, lest his deeds should be exposed."

Is your behavior one way when the light of family or peers shines brightly on your life... and another way when that light is absent? Do you talk the same when you are off on that business trip as you do when you are at a church meeting or at home? Do you watch the "usual" television programs when you are alone in that motel room? Do you hold the same moral standard consistently at home or when you are away?

The truth is that far too many men indulge in private sins that would devastate their family if the truth were known. I have seen families destroyed when they discovered that the husband and father who appeared godly when at home was nurturing some secret sin when on the road. On a Christian radio talk show a woman called in to tell of her husband's 22-year secret of pornography and prostitution. He was one man with her and the children and another man when he was absent from them.

Men, integrity is moral soundness and purity. Integrity means we are the same whether anyone is watching or not because integrity is at the very core of who we are.

Do you have someone you can talk with about your private sins?

Little Sly Foxes

Song of Solomon 2:15: "Catch the foxes for us, the little foxes that are ruining the vineyards, while our vineyards are in blossom."

The little foxes in this story could be in reference to what we might consider to be "small" sins that linger in our lives and erode our fruitfulness. While *all* sin is hideous before God, needing the blood of Christ for cleansing and forgiveness, we tend to regard some sins as more serious than others. There are sins we take lightly (which I think God does not) that are robbing us of life and diminish our integrity. They are cracks or flaws in our moral soundness.

* * *

Several years ago I applied for a part-time position at a telemarketing firm. The job was to call residents to collect data. During the training we were told to say, "I was out in your neighborhood yesterday and missed you at home so I'm following up my visit with a phone call." I told the trainer I could not say that because it wasn't true. The trainer said, "Donovan, if you have a problem saying it the way we tell you, perhaps you are not our caliber of person." I said, "I guess I'm not." I looked elsewhere for work.

I went to real estate school and got a license to sell real estate. One of my early sales involved going to the bank with a couple to help them with their loan process. The banker told us he could not give them the loan on this home unless the lawn was seeded. He turned to me and said, "Go get a bale of straw, spread some on the lawn, take a picture, and sign this form stating that the lawn was seeded." I couldn't do it. He had to get someone else.

* * *

Those two encounters alone, and I could share numerous other illustrations, revealed to me how often men are tempted to compromise in what may seem to be insignificant ways. Someone once told me that he heard J.R. on the television series *Dallas* say that once you compromise in even the smallest thing the rest of life is a piece of cake. J.R. was speaking a dangerous truth. Small compromises are giant steps toward destructive sin. Daily those compromises face us. Whether it be inaccurate reporting for income taxes, exceeding the speed limit, or telling our children to tell that salesman that we are not home, our integrity is jeopardized when we compromise.

It is true that none of us will achieve moral perfection in this life, but we must be about the pursuit of holiness. We must press on to be pure, moral men of integrity. No sin is insignificant because sin falls short of God's very best for us.

Can you think of some "little foxes" that have crept into your life, bringing compromise and destructive sin?

The Road To The Liberty Bowl

How do we overcome those secret sins of the heart, mind, and private moments? How do we deal with those "little foxes" that run rampant in our lives and flaw the fruit of our integrity? Let me suggest three things you can do to get on the road to liberty.

1. Confess Your Sin.

> **Psalm 32:3-5:** "When I kept silent about my sin, my body wasted away through my groaning all day long. For day and night thy hand was heavy upon me; my vitality was drained away as with the fever heat of summer. I acknowledged my sin to thee, and my iniquity I did not hide; I said, 'I will confess my transgressions to the Lord'; and thou didst forgive the guilt of my sin."

> **1 John 1:9:** "If we confess our sins, he is faithful and righteous to forgive us our sins and to cleanse us from all unrighteousness."

> **James 5:16a:** "Therefore, confess your sins to one another, and pray for one another, so that you may be healed."

121

Own up to your sin. Don't make excuses. Admit your sin to yourself, to others who care about you, and to God. The first step in overcoming any sin is acknowledging that the sin is there.

2. Accountability Is Essential.

> **2 Samuel 12:7-9:** "Nathan then said to David, 'You are the man! Thus says the Lord God of Israel, "It is I who anointed you king over Israel and it is I who delivered you from the hand of Saul. I also gave you your master's house and your master's wives into your care, and I gave you the house of Israel and Judah; and if that had been too little, I would have added to you many more things like these! Why have you despised the word of the Lord by doing evil in his sight? You have struck down Uriah the Hittite with the sword, have taken his wife to be your wife, and have killed him with the sword of the sons of Ammon." ' "

King David was wise enough to have men around him who would speak into his life. Do you have anyone who will hold you accountable? Do you have a trusted friend to whom you can tell of even your secret sins? Accountability works as a security fence to keep us on the right path.

3. Repentance Reaps Refreshment.

> **Acts 3:19:** "Repent therefore and return, that your sins may be wiped away, in order that times of refreshing may come from the presence of the Lord."

To repent means to have a change of mind... and actions. Resolve that you are going to turn from your sin and do things differently. I have seen many men overcome sin simply by changing some of their life-patterns.

The young man who struggled with pornography stopped going into establishments that sold it and found liberty. A young couple who

122

realized they were going too far physically in their relationship resolved to not be alone for long periods of time. They kept themselves sexually pure for their wedding day. The young businessman who often got drunk on trips out of town decided to make regular calls home to keep himself accountable. These are examples of true repentance that led to refreshing integrity.

In Conclusion

Integrity is such a valuable asset in our lives. As we walk in integrity we avoid the ravages of the destructive nature of sin. We ensure a strong, shining witness for Christ as others see our good works and glorify God, our heavenly Father. We set a sound example before our peers and family of obedience unto Christ. Most of all, our integrity pleases and honors God.

> "Has the Lord as much delight in burnt offerings and sacrifices as in obeying the voice of the Lord? Behold, to obey is better than sacrifice, and to heed than the fat of rams."
> 1 Samuel 15:22

Walking This Out...

I am convinced that integrity is a heart issue, not a behavior issue. We can change our behaviors and still have a dark spot in our hearts. I've seen men who have seemingly taken all the right steps, put all the safeguards in place, yet fallen into some devious sin that shocked even those closest to them.

That said, setting the heart to live an authentic life before God and man is crucial to walking this out. You must resolve that there will be no secret sins.

Intimacy with God is the greatest safeguard I know to personal integrity. When you really come to grips with who you are in Christ, and who God is, it will transform everything and will serve as a guard over your integrity.

Because I know God knows all, sees all, that I answer to him and that he desires better for me than I do myself it impacts every thought, word, and action.

If you want to live a life of integrity, live a life of intimacy with God... and with others.

Next Session

We have discussed integrity with several references to sexual purity. In our next session we will deal specifically with biblical principles about sex. The Bible has much to say about the subject. Sex is a wonderful gift of God to bring both pleasure and procreation.

Session 11

My Body — His Temple

(Sexual purity)

My Body Is His

1 Corinthians 6:19-20: "Or do you not know that your body is a temple of the Holy Spirit who is in you, whom you have from God, and that you are not your own? For you have been bought with a price; therefore glorify God in your body."

Paul's letters to the church at Corinth reflect more comments about sexual matters than any of his other letters. The Corinthian Christians, it seems, had some problems in that area. Paul wrote these words to them: "It is actually reported that there is immorality among you, and immorality of such a kind as does not exist even among the Gentiles (unbelievers), that someone has his father's wife" (1 Corinthians 5:1).

There are a few theories as to what was the source of the Corinthian carnality. It may have been a notion of "cheap grace." Cheap grace allows one to say to himself, "I'm not under the law anymore... God will forgive me when I sin." New Testament Christians as well as contemporary Christians have been confused into thinking that somehow grace allows us to be irresponsible regarding sin.

Another theory for the problems at Corinth revolves around a misunderstanding of the relationship of the body and the Spirit. There seems to have been the belief that what one did with one's body had little to do with the spiritual condition. That belief is what Paul addresses head-on with his admonition, "Your body is a temple of the Holy Spirit. You are not your own!" It does matter what you do with your body. There is a binding relationship between the physical and the spiritual.

As we candidly discuss sexual issues, let us begin with this fundamental, foundational premise that our body is not our own. It is his! We are a temple of the Holy Spirit and our physical participations affect our spiritual maturation. Let us, therefore, glorify God in our body. When it comes to sexual activity, what best pleases God, glorifying him and expressing his character and will?

Do you think you grasp the concept that your body is a temple of the Holy Spirit and what you do with your body does matter?

The Marriage Bed

> **Hebrews 13:4:** "Let marriage be held in honor among all, and let the marriage bed be undefiled; for fornicators and adulterers God will judge."

Since God introduced Adam to Eve and joined them as one, marriage has been a precious priority on the heart of God. The marital union of a man and a woman is a gift of intimacy, pleasure, and growth for both participants. The fact that the Bible uses marital pictures to describe our relationship with God through Jesus Christ ought to tip us off as to how important marriage is to God.

In the American culture is marriage held in honor? Fifty percent of marriages end in divorce. Of the 50% who stay together, how many enjoy an intimate, life-giving relationship? Have we who belong to Christ sought to keep the marriage bed undefiled? Let us consider some actions and attitudes that will express an honoring of marriage, promoting an undefiled marriage bed of sexual purity.

1. Sacrificial Sex Life

> **Ephesians 5:25:** "Husbands, love your wives, just as Christ also loved the church and gave himself up for her."

Men, we say we love our wives, but how often are we willing to love them enough to be self-sacrificing in our sexual relationship? How often do we put our own sexual desires above the needs and desires of our wives? Do we try to be sensitive and understanding to the male-female differences when it comes to sexual attitudes? Loving your wife as Christ loved the church means seeking to identify with her humanity and being willing to lay down your own life to enrich her life. In a nutshell, sacrificial love means putting the needs of your wife ahead of your own.

The Bible has never advocated that women be objects of our sexual gratification, yet men throughout the centuries have painfully dishonored women by regarding them as sex objects.

* * *

Several years ago during the so-called sexual revolution, I heard a report on the news of a survey that had been done on college campuses. They asked sexually active college students why they had chosen not to wait until marriage to engage in sexual intercourse. Over 90% of the young women responded, "Because I love him." Among the men surveyed, over 90% said, "Because I love it." Certainly we see a dramatic contrast.

* * *

As men, we tend to see sexual intercourse as something we "do" while women view it as intimate, interpersonal expression. The sex-crazy women you see in the television sitcoms and movies generally do not exist. (Usually they flow from the creative pen of a male scriptwriter!)

Women long for security, affection, and communication which foster intimate sexual activity. The fact that *Playboy* magazine is the number one best-seller among men, while *Better Homes and Gardens* is the number one magazine for women is a clear reflection of how men and women approach sexual relationships differently. As

129

Christian men, let us strive for the high standard to lay down our own lives sacrificially and honor our wives by putting their needs first.

2. Mutual Consent

> **Ephesians 5:21:** "Be subject to one another in the fear of Christ."

> **1 Corinthians 7:4:** "The wife does not have authority over her own body, but the husband does; and likewise also the husband does not have authority over his own body, but the wife does."

A book that was extremely helpful to my wife and me as sexually inexperienced newlyweds was Dr. Ed Wheat's book, *Intended for Pleasure*. (I got excited with the title alone!) In Dr. Wheat's book I saw such respect for the marriage relationship with solid counsel on keeping the marriage bed undefiled. His book helped both Elaine and me to see sexual intercourse as God's intention for mutual intimacy and pleasure.

While sex is to be enjoyed fully, are there sexual activities that are not appropriate even in the context of marriage? A non-Christian marriage counselor told me once that he felt that "anything goes" as long as both parties consent. Let's consider some guidelines for a God-honoring, spouse-honoring sex life in our marriage.

Mutual consent is an important ingredient to maintaining purity in our sexual activity. As a rule, I would encourage you to avoid any activity that makes your wife emotionally or physically uncomfortable. Nothing should be done that might degrade her.

How do you know what makes her feel uncomfortable? Ask her! I talked with a couple once who were struggling in their sexual relationship. For the first time, after several years of marriage, she told her husband that sexual intercourse was very painful for her.

He was stunned. It turned out to be a medical problem that could be corrected. The real issue, however, was that there had not been the ability to discuss "sex" in their marriage. Ask your wife what gives her greatest pleasure. Ask her if there is anything that makes her uncomfortable or makes her feel dishonored. Communication moves us toward mutual consent, which fosters honor, intimacy, and pleasure in the marriage bed.

For Christians, however, mutual consent is more than two-sided. Christ is involved. We are to submit to one another in the fear of Christ. I do not believe that anything goes as long as both consent. What if you both consent to partner-swapping with the neighbors? What if you consent to physical torture or other perversions? Does that honor Christ? When I speak of mutual consent for the Christian, I am talking about a three-way agreement, with Christ at the head.

Have you ever asked your wife if there is anything in your sexual activity that makes her feel uncomfortable?

3. Agreeable Abstinence

> **1 Corinthians 7:5:** "Stop depriving one another, except by agreement for a time, that you may devote yourselves to prayer, and come together again lest Satan tempt you because of your lack of self-control."

There are times when it is appropriate to agree to refrain from sexual activity in the marriage. Here in Corinthians, Paul gives the reason of devotion to prayer. What a beautiful season in the marriage when the husband and wife are so intimate and united in prayer that they mutually agree to abstain from sexual intercourse. During this "fast" from sexual activity the couple is in a place to focus clearly on the purposes of God.

Is prayer the only appropriate reason to consent mutually to abstain from sexual intercourse? Because godly marital sex is self-sacrificing and in mutual submission, there are occasions when refraining from intercourse is justified.

There is a season after the birth of a child when it is mutually wise to refrain from intercourse. There can be other expressions of sexual activity, but intercourse probably should be avoided. Consult your physician if you have questions about when to resume normal sexual activity. Keep in mind that your wife has not only experienced great physical trauma, including hormonal, but also emotional trauma. To bring honor to the marriage union, this is usually a good time to agree mutually to abstain.

During the woman's menstrual period may be another occasion to agree mutually to refrain from intercourse. Remember men, menstruation does not merely affect your wife physically, but emotionally as well. Be willing to walk in agreement to refrain.

There are times when either of you may be ill, emotionally worn, or physically exhausted which may call for a season of agreement to abstain from sexual activity. The key to mutual agreement is healthy communication and genuine concern for one another.

Marriages get into trouble when either the husband or the wife decides alone when there will be sexual intercourse and when there will not. The wife is not to use the withdrawal of sex as a tool to punish her husband as the television sitcoms so often portray. The husband must not attempt to get revenge on his wife by refusing to have intercourse with her. I knew of one marriage in which the husband had moved to a separate bedroom and told his wife they would only have sex when he came to her. He was "punishing" her for something she had done.

Sexual intercourse is a beautiful, intimate sharing of oneness. That oneness is to be mutually enjoyed — and only mutually excluded.

4. Fantasy Free

Proverbs 5:15-19: "Drink water from your own cistern and fresh water from your own well. Should your springs be dispersed abroad, streams of water in the streets? Let them be yours alone and not for strangers with you. Let your fountain be blessed, and rejoice in the wife of your youth. As a loving hind and a graceful doe, let her breasts satisfy you at all times; be exhilarated always with her love."

You do not need sexual stimulation from any other source than your wife. When the scripture says, "Drink water from your own cistern, and fresh water from your own well," it is not talking about water. It is talking about sexual satisfaction. You dishonor your wife and defile the marriage bed when you invite fantasy to provide sexual gratification.

The wife who has discovered her husband's addiction to pornography is most grieved by the fact that he seems to prefer the picture of another woman over the reality of her presence. If your sex life requires pornographic stimulation for you to achieve satisfaction, let me encourage you to seek godly counsel. God intends for the wife he gave you to be your source of sexual exhilaration.

* * *

A few months before Elaine and I were engaged, I struggled with how I was sexually exhilarated in her presence. I wasn't sure if my struggle was temptation, lust, or normal attraction. I fasted and prayed and sought counsel from God. I believe that he reminded me of these verses in Proverbs, "Let her breasts satisfy you at all times; be exhilarated always with her love." He was giving me encouragement of how good marital sex was going to be. I shared these verses with Elaine (after we were engaged), and she blushed. I told her I thought the verses were awesome. They said to me that I would find my sexual delight in her — and in her alone. That is exactly

how it has been all of our married years. I do not
need any other well to draw from!

* * *

If you struggle with finding sexual satisfaction in your wife alone,
talk openly with her about it. Seek godly counsel together. Hold your
marriage in a place of honor and keep that marriage bed undefiled.

5. Dedicated To God

> **1 Corinthians 6:20:** "For you have been bought with a price;
> therefore, glorify God in your body."

A marriage that is honorable and undefiled is one that is dedicated to
God. Like the Corinthians, too often we see sex as something purely
physical, separate from our spiritual life. The two are directly connected.

Sexual intercourse is a beautiful gift from God. He so designed the
body (male and female) to be a perfect fit that would produce tremendous physical pleasure. He made something great! It has been
man's perversion and promiscuity that has brought sorrow and destruction.

Because your sex life is a gift from God, seek his counsel as to how
it is to be all that he wants it to be. Pray together for God to bless
your marriage bed and to show you how to keep it undefiled. Men, if
it has been defiled, turn to the one who can forgive and cleanse. He
will give you a new start!

When it comes to a sex life dedicated to God there is one other issue I would call you to consider. Far more couples are deciding to
have no children. I officiated at a marriage where the couple recently
made it clear that children did not fit into their future dreams. I asked
them if they had prayed about that. They replied that they had not.
It amazes me the number of Christian couples I have met who will

pray about where to live, what job to do, what car to buy, but think they do not need the counsel of God regarding birth control. May your marriage bed be totally consecrated to God, walking in full submission to him.

Sex And The Single Man

It is difficult for the single man in our day who chooses to keep himself pure. Our culture shouts messages of self-gratification and sexual stimulation. Fifty percent of couples are choosing to move in together rather than marry. Homosexuality is elevated to a position of normalcy; in fact it is promoted by some as God's design. Internet porn, television, movies, and magazines trigger sexual fantasies that lead to lust, and lust gives way to sinful sexual activity. What is a Christian single man to do to stand against the tide of sexual promiscuity?

1. Stand On The Truth!

The world promotes a lie that God's standards for sexual activity are unfair and restrictive. Society cries, "God just doesn't want us to have any fun!" The truth is that God has set the standards to guard us because of his great love for us. He put up fences not to take away our joy but to ensure it.

* * *

Mark and Angie had been dating for several months before they decided to move in together. They thought a trial period would be good for them. They practiced "safe sex," carefully using a condom each time they had intercourse. When Angie missed her period they both were in shock. The doctor confirmed their fears. Angie was pregnant. What would they do? Both were in college with careers ahead. A baby was so inconvenient right now. They wished they had listened to Mark's brother who told them of God's design for a relationship. He had even told them the fact that condoms have a 6-15% fail rate, but they didn't believe him. They had bought the "safe sex" lie and the standards of the culture.

* * *

2. Flee Sexual Sin

As a single man you must set up safeguards to keep yourself pure. Here are a few tips to staying on top of your sexual temptations.

1. Be faithful to pray daily and read the Bible devotionally. Singleness is a great time to press in on your intimacy with God.

2. Stay in good fellowship with other Christians. Walk close with gals and guys who hold the same values of sexual purity.

3. Have an accountability partner you can trust.

4. Have an open relationship with your pastor.

5. Avoid sexually stimulating films and magazines. It's not good to fire up the engines without a proper route to run on.

6. Avoid lengthy opportunities alone with the opposite sex.

7. Have clear guidelines of how far is too far in relationships. Look to the scriptures in setting those boundaries.

Remaining sexually pure in this culture is not an easy task for a single man. You can enjoy the freedom of sexual purity by the strength Christ will give you and the support from fellow Christians.

Can you think of other safeguards a single Christian can employ to keep himself sexually pure?

The Gay Revolution

There is great confusion in our culture regarding homosexuality with conflicting messages coming from the political arena, from the scientific and medical community, and even from the church. There is no question that many men struggle with the issue of homosexuality, even Christian men. Judgmentalism, homophobia, accusation, alienation, and violence do not reflect the heart of Christ on this matter.

God's word is truth, and he addressed this issue. He inspired the Apostle Paul to write these words to a culture that was so much like ours:

> "For this reason God gave them up to dishonorable passions. For their women exchanged natural relations for those that are contrary to nature; and the men likewise gave up natural relations with women and were consumed with passion for one another, men committing shameless acts with men and receiving in themselves the due penalty for their error."
> Romans 1:26-27

Nearly 2,000 years ago the Roman culture looked much like ours is becoming and scriptures give God's gracious warning of the result.

* * *

My wife and I teach fourth and fifth graders at our church's children's program. One Wednesday our kids seemed unsettled. I asked, "What's going on with you all?" Immediately one of the students said, "We got the sex talk at school today." Another piped in, "Yeah, our teacher told us homosexuality is normal... that people are born that way." Because we had a mixed group I did not pursue the topic further, but told them to be sure to talk with their parents when they got home that evening.

As I thought about that teacher's comments, I wish I could have been a fifth grader to ask, "So how do two homosexual men have normal sex?" I wonder if the teacher would have told them about oral sex, anal intercourse, rimming or fisting, attempting to describe those as normal behaviors.

* * *

Sin is anything that falls short of God's best for us. God wants much more for us. Everything God gives spells life with a capital "L" and every counterfeit the devil offers spells death. God made sex perfect and wonderful, fulfilling and fruitful, in the holy and pure context of a man and a woman in covenant relationship.

Wanting to be cautiously conservative, studies have shown that homosexual males have a life expectancy anywhere from three to twenty years less than heterosexual males. Homosexual sex is high risk — even dangerous. I think that is what the Holy Spirit was showing Paul as he wrote to the Romans.

The real issue, however, is one of identity. That has been the devil's tactic since the beginning. Doesn't he constantly call into question for all of us, "Who do you think you are?" And to the guy struggling with his sexual identity a voice whispers, "You are gay. God made you that way. You can't change."

I knew a young man who was tender and sensitive. Because of that he often was ridiculed. I believe God made that young man a tender soul who would have been an amazing husband or a father who really nurtured his children. But he bought the lie and died of AIDS at the age of 21.

So what if homosexuality is your struggle? Like any other temptation that comes our way, God has provided a way out (1 Corinthians 10:13). Talk to your pastor or to a trusted Christian friend. Call it sin just as God does and deal with it that way. Be willing to repent.

Dig deep in your relationship with Jesus. He is the answer to all bondage. He brings freedom and life. Jesus is the source of our true identity.

Immerse yourself in the truth. Don't feed the lie; feed God's truth about who you are. If or when you stumble, get up again and keep returning to the cross. Jason Gray wrote a powerful song, "Remind Me Who I Am." Let the Holy Spirit remind you who you are.

A Word About Masturbation

There are both single and married men who wrestle with masturbation. Is it sin? Is it a normal release of sexual pressure? Christendom is divided on the matter with some who would say masturbation is always sin to those who would say it is very normal behavior not to be discouraged. Then there are those moderately somewhere in the middle.

It is very clear that when masturbation is accompanied with lust and perverse thoughts it is sinful. When a man finds himself habitually addicted to masturbating, having lost self-control, clearly the habit falls short of God's best for him. When a husband finds sexual exhilaration from self-stimulus rather than from the wife of his youth, he has missed God's design for his sexual satisfaction. Often actions or attitudes related to masturbation fall short of God's best for us. What is going on in your heart and mind is the real issue when it comes to masturbation.

Masturbation is common among men. Guilt and frustration also are common with masturbation, especially among Christian men. Ask God to search your heart regarding attitudes or actions associated with masturbation. Seek out counsel from a trusted Christian friend or a pastor. When the Holy Spirit brings conviction, respond appropriately. Confess your sin. Ask God to forgive and cleanse. Receive his forgiveness and repent, turning from that for which you received conviction. Remember, you are to glorify God in your body, so seek to live in such a way that will best honor God.

In Conclusion

Sex is a difficult topic, especially for men. We are so enamored with it. Our sexual thoughts and actions are often spiritual battlegrounds. Keep in mind that sex is a good gift from God to be enjoyed at the proper time with the proper guidelines, in the context of marriage. You will find the greatest delight in keeping God's standard and he will receive the greatest glory.

Walking This Out...

Sexual purity is a difficult pursuit for every man I know. Because we are visually stimulated, we must constantly be on our guard.

I am blessed with the word I heard God say and a wonderful wife who fulfills that word. I believe that is God's intention for every man. But that does not mean I am not in the struggle with every other man.

It means I am careful what I see. Men, you can turn away. And when it comes to pornography, even the so-called "soft-porn," don't allow yourself to go there.

I also guard my alone times. There was a time when I would travel alone, get to my hotel, and immediately turn on the TV. I discovered quickly you can get sucked in to some raunchy stuff. I am grateful for my laptop and iPad (and Netflix) so I can control what I watch. Often I just crank up worship music!

I avoid being alone with the opposite sex. I don't share heart issues with women other than my wife. I do not give frontal hugs to anyone other than my wife.

Men, boundaries provide freedom and safety!

Next Session

The Apostle Paul wrote that "the love of money is a root of all sorts of evil" (1 Timothy 6:10). The Bible has much to say about finances and how to handle money properly. Next session we are going to take a look at some foundational financial principles found in God's word.

Session 12

Firm Financial Foundations

(It's all His!)

Mastering Money

1 Timothy 6:10-11: "For the love of money is a root of all sorts of evil, and some by longing for it have wandered away from the faith, and pierced themselves with many a pang. But flee from these things, you man of God; and pursue righteousness, godliness, faith, love, perseverance, and gentleness."

Have you been pierced with many a pang pursuing pennies? Has the love of money caused a wrestling in your life, causing you to wander away from the faith? Money and other things of this world have a strong allure to become central in our lives. Too often we buy the lie that if we just had more "stuff" we would have more happiness, peace, and contentment. Jesus is to be Lord of every area of our lives, including our finances, and he is the source of our peace, joy, and contentment.

Matthew 6:24: "No one can serve two masters; for either he will hate the one and love the other, or he will hold to one and despise the other. You cannot serve God and mammon (money)."

Money is not a problem in and of itself. When we struggle with the love of money the real issue is a heart problem. Who is master of our lives? Are our hearts surrendered to God, allowing him to give the directives in all aspects of our lives?

A master or lord is the one who gives the orders. He guides and motivates those in subjection to him. Does God guide and motivate your life... or does the pursuit of material gain? Do you do what you do because you know it is what God wants or because it seems like the best way to make money?

* * *

> While attending a pastors' conference a few years ago, I heard one of the speakers pose a piercing question. "If money were not an issue, is there anything you would be doing differently with your life?" Nearly all of us agreed that our pursuits would change. I said I would love to be an author, but I have great fear of starvation and seeing my children naked. Is it possible that our passion for financial security could cause us to miss the will of God for our lives? Who or what is guiding and motivating your life?

* * *

Understand that there are times we must be involved in labors that we do not cherish to maintain the priority of providing for our families. God does not excuse irresponsibility. We must, however, prayerfully seek the heart of God as to whether we have compromised and missed the master's directives and fallen prey to a passion for possessions.

Careful Caretakers

> **Genesis 1:28:** "And God blessed them; and God said to them, 'Be fruitful and multiply, and fill the earth, and subdue it; and rule over the fish of the sea and over the birds of the sky, and over every living thing that moves on the earth.'"

From the beginning, God put man on planet earth as a caretaker of all the "stuff" that is here. It all belongs to God, but he has entrusted us to manage and care for his creation. A term we use often in the church is the word "steward." A steward is a manager or overseer. We are to be good stewards of God's creation.

In the area of finances we are called to be good stewards, faithful caretakers of God's provision. We must remember, it is all his and we are entrusted to administrate well what he has given to us. We maintain a healthy biblical perspective when we remember that we are God's careful caretakers of his precious provision.

* * *

I served a rural church for seven years in Northwest Missouri. Those farmers taught me much about faith and stewardship. One older farmer told me of the day he made his final mortgage payment. (That's a big deal for a farmer!) He walked out into the center of his fields and boasted to himself, "It's all mine!" As soon as he had uttered those words he sensed the Spirit of the Lord speak back to him, saying, "That's what the last owner said too. Remember my son, it's all mine!" The farmer fell to his knees and wept. His tears were a mixture of both remorse and gratitude. He was sorry for his arrogance and grateful for God's gentle hand to put things back in perspective.

* * *

Do you understand your role as a steward?

Fatal Financial Flaws

John 10:10: "The thief comes only to steal, and kill and destroy; I came that they might have life, and might have it abundantly."

Jesus came to give us life in every area of our lives, including our finances. If we are to be good and fruitful stewards of the things of God, we cannot allow the thief (Satan) to steal, kill, and destroy even our material possessions.

I do not mean that God wants us rich. I am not proclaiming a gospel of financial prosperity. There is a principle of fruitfulness and life that permeates the scriptures. Whether we have little or much, God desires good fruit to come from what we have. In the realm of our finances we are to experience the reality of "life-giving," rather than life-consuming. Money and other material possessions are to be utilized as godly tools to see the kingdom of God extended. Money can provide great avenues to glorify God, as well as meet your basic human needs.

The reality is that far too many Christians find themselves in frequent financial crisis: debt, worry, and covetousness (craving what we do not have) plague our attitudes and actions. Even leaders in Christian ministry have crumbled under the pressure the love of money exerts. Why do so many get into financial bondage and disarray, leading to frustration and fruitlessness?

In my years in the pastorate I have observed several causes for financial failure among God's people. Here are some that occur most often.

1. Failure to have a budget or maintain one defeats many. A budget is a financial target that keeps us on course to achieve godly goals. If we have no budget we most certainly will miss the mark of being fruitful stewards. If we have a budget, but ignore it, we are no better off. If you want to walk in financial freedom, the place to begin is for you and your spouse to establish a God-guided budget and live by it.

Do you have a realistic, workable budget that you live by?

2. "Keeping up with the Joneses" lures many of us into financial difficulties. We want the latest iPhone, iPad, car, home, or whatever it is that the neighbors just got. Peer pressure doesn't only work on teens. We often ignore our budget or the prompting of the Holy Spirit because we are seeking to maintain the latest trends.

What purchases have you made that were motivated by peer pressure?

3. Poor planning plagues many. Property taxes come due every year, yet how many people seem surprised by them? Your car will need new tires some day. Why do I hear Christians say, "We're really in a crunch right now, we had to buy new tires!" We can anticipate many expenses and set aside provision for them. Plan ahead!

4. Are you an "impulse" consumer? Before we got on a budget I would always come out of the store with something that was not on my list. When the telemarketing person calls, are you prone to making hasty purchases? Impulse spending can set your finances into total disarray.

What was your latest impulse purchase?

5. Credit cards come too easy and are too easy to use. Debt, especially incurred on a credit card, is bondage. The bill always comes due. If you do not fully anticipate the ability to pay off that credit card each month, you must seriously consider the appropriateness of its usage.

I have seen far too many young couples, and some older couples, over their heads in debt because of easy credit card access. Watch out for the credit card trap!

6. Discerning needs from wants is a struggle for us all. A key to financial stability is the ability to distinguish needs from wants. I have seen people who have a difficult time getting food on the table, yet they keep their cable television bill current or zip into McDonald's on a regular basis. Have you diligently sought to distinguish your needs from your wants?

7. Sinful habits can bring havoc to your financial health. Overeating, purchasing illegal drugs, gambling, or addiction to pornography are just a few sinful habits that are costly and erosive to the family finances. Failure to use finances according to biblical directives, such as tithing, can bring financial instability. Sin has a high price, both spiritually and materially.

8. One of the greatest hindrances to financial freedom and stability is the failure to put God's will first.

"But seek first his kingdom and his righteousness; and all these things shall be added to you."
Matthew 6:33

We get into financial messes many times simply because we did not pray prior to an economic decision. Every time we ignore the counsel of God, we become vulnerable to loss.

Can you tell of a time you regretted a financial decision because of your failure to pray?

Solving The Financial Slump

Solutions necessarily relate specifically to the problems. Let us consider ten tips that will move us toward financial stability.

1. Set up a budget and live by it. If you have trouble getting started with the budget process, let me suggest that you visit the website of Crown Financial Ministries (crown.org) and order *The Financial Planning Organizer*. My family has faithfully functioned with this budget system with great success. Be sure your budget is realistic and mutually acceptable. When you get a budget developed, resolve to live by it. It will be a difficult discipline at first, but it will lead to financial freedom in the long run.

2. Just say "no" to peer pressure when it comes to those unplanned expenditures. Don't covet any of your neighbor's belongings and don't sabotage your budget to get what your neighbor has.

3. Plan ahead for those large expenditures. We set aside $50 per month for Christmas gifts. We put $100 per month in savings for property tax and insurance. I met with a couple once and suggested they set aside $40 per month for their car insurance. They said they couldn't afford to do that. I asked them if they could afford the $500 on January 1, when the premium came due. They admitted that the insurance payment always sent them into a financial tailspin and forced them to live on credit cards. Credit is not the solution! Planning and laying aside the provision within our means is the key.

4. Never exceed your budget. Resist impulsive purchases. Having a budget has made it easy for me to say to those telemarketing agents that what they are promoting doesn't fit within our budget. It also keeps me focused when I go into any store.

5. If you cannot control yourself when it comes to credit cards, then I suggest that you destroy them. Debt is bondage. Credit cards, however, are not the real problem. The person signing the ticket is the problem.

* * *

> We use a credit card that has no annual fee and pays a percentage per purchase. Each time we use the credit card we record it in our checkbook and subtract it from our balance just as if we had written a check. When I pay the credit card bill, I have nothing to subtract, pay no interest, and receive a monthly bonus. Annually we receive a check for $200 or more for using our credit card.

* * *

Just as money is not the root of all evil, credit cards are not the root of financial bondage.

6. You can prepare for crisis. Set money aside for car repairs, home repairs, medical emergencies (including insurance deductibles), or a layoff from work. We replaced the transmission in our van recently, and because we had been setting aside $50 each month, we were able to write out a check for the repair, avoiding financial crisis. Let me suggest a goal of six months salary in savings to hedge against potential layoff. While we cannot anticipate every crisis, nor should we become so self-reliant we forsake dependency upon God, good planning for potential crisis is wisdom.

7. Be a smart shopper. When making a major purchase, take your time and do your homework. Consult a reliable financial publication such as Consumer Reports. Remember, cheapest is not always best. Measure your decision by more than just dollars and cents. Do not be afraid to buy secondhand. Generally, the greatest margin of profit is built into the purchase of an item when it is new.

8. Prioritize your spending according to biblical guidelines. Needs come before wants. Prayerfully let God have leadership in your finances.

9. Repent of sinful habits that are robbing you of financial stability. Seek counsel from your pastor or other spiritual advisor as to what portions of your income might be going to items that do not glorify God or bring life to you and your family. You may need to seek assistance to overcome destructive habits that are eroding your financial security.

10. Seek first the kingdom of God and his righteousness. I heard a preacher say one time that he had baptized many men who testified to total surrender to Christ, but not one of them got baptized with his billfold in his pocket. Not that men should get their billfolds wet. What the preacher was saying was that too often he saw a failure to surrender totally to God when it comes to finances. It is not easy to surrender.

Do you remember the story of the rich young ruler who came to Jesus asking about salvation? Let's take a look at it.

> **Matthew 19:16-26:** "And behold, one came to him and said, 'Teacher, what good thing shall I do that I may obtain eternal life?' And he said to him, 'Why are you asking me about what is good? There is only one who is good; but if you wish

to enter into life, keep the commandments.' He said to him, 'Which ones?' And Jesus said, 'You shall not commit murder; you shall not commit adultery; you shall not steal; you shall not bear false witness; honor your father and mother; and you shall love your neighbor as yourself.' The young man said to him, 'All these things I have kept; what am I still lacking?' Jesus said to him, 'If you wish to be complete, go and sell your possessions and give to the poor and you shall have treasure in heaven; and come follow me.' But when the young man heard this statement, he went away grieved; for he was one who owned much property. And Jesus said to his disciples, 'Truly I say to you, it is easier for a camel to go through the eye of a needle, than for a rich man to enter the kingdom of God.' And when the disciples heard this, they were very astonished and said, 'Then who can be saved?' And looking upon them Jesus said to them, 'With men this is impossible, but with God all things are possible.' "

Notice that the disciples said, "Then who can be saved?" They were saying that a passion for riches was a struggle for all of us. While many of us may never have riches or be considered rich, all of us will wrestle from time to time with our love affair with money and other material things. Seeking first the kingdom of God and his righteousness is a daily resolve that leads to life and liberty.

Which of the ten suggestions did you find most helpful? Most challenging?

Give And Live!

Luke 6:38: "Give, and it will be given to you; good measure, pressed down, shaken together, running over, they will pour into your lap. For whatever measure you deal out to others, it will be dealt to you in return."

2 Corinthians 9:6-7: "Now this I say, he who sows sparingly shall also reap sparingly; and he who sows bountifully shall also reap bountifully. Let each one do just as he has purposed in his heart; not grudgingly or under compulsion; for God loves a cheerful giver."

When I was a church planter we conducted a city-wide survey, knocking on over 2,000 doors. We asked people why they thought folks who did not go to church did not go. The number two answer was, "Because the church is always asking for money!" It is a sad commentary on the church that there is a tremendous amount of fund-raisers, special offerings, or building funds that keep people inundated with requests. It is also tragic in our day that the average giving to the church is about 1-3% of our income, depending upon which survey you read.

Giving is an important part of maintaining a spiritually healthy attitude toward finances. The Bible has much to say about giving, including the encouragement to tithe faithfully.

A Word About Tithing

Malachi 3:10: " 'Bring the whole tithe into the storehouse, so that there may be food in my house, and test me now in this,' says the Lord of hosts, 'if I will not open for you the windows of heaven, and pour out for you a blessing until there is no more need.' "

What is tithing and is it intended for Christians today? The word *tithe* is defined in *Unger's Bible Dictionary.*

Tithe, from the Greek word, *dekate*; a tenth. In Mosaic Law the tenth of all produce, flocks, and cattle was declared to be sacred to Jehovah.

When Malachi said, "Bring the whole tithe into the storehouse," he was speaking of 10% of the firstfruits of one's labor. The biblical percentage has not changed.

Jesus affirmed tithing in his statement to the Pharisees:

Matthew 23:23: "Woe to you, scribes and Pharisees, hypocrites! For you tithe mint and dill and cumin, and have neglected the weightier provisions of the law; justice and mercy and faithfulness; but these are the things you should have done without neglecting the others."

While Jesus gave a strong admonition regarding the Pharisees' neglect of justice, mercy, and faithfulness, he gave no provision for the neglect of the basics, such as tithing. Jesus does give a clear call to do whatever we do with a pure heart and a desire to honor God first.

Some seem to believe that tithing ended with the New Covenant and grace. In a sense, it did. Christians did not just give 10%... they gave all (Acts 2:45). We hear the excuse in our day, however, that "I don't have to tithe. We are under grace!" Grace is never an excuse to do less. It is always a call to more... to a higher standard. Jesus did not come to do away with the law, but to fulfill (Matthew 5:17). He takes us beyond the law. He challenges us to go the second mile... to give not only our coat, but our shirt also. Tithing is just a starting place in the joyous art of cheerful giving!

Giving is something we get to do, not that we've got to do. It comes from a grateful heart that has received much from a loving Father, God. Remember, the nature of God is to give. "For God so loved the world, he gave"! As those who have been created in his likeness and who are being conformed to the image of his Son, we too will be vessels of joyful generosity.

In Conclusion

The real issue with money is a matter of the heart. Jesus said, "Where your treasure is, there will your heart be also" (Matthew 6:21). Where is your treasure? Where is your heart? Are your finances established around biblical parameters? In all that we say, do, and are, our passion is to please God and honor him, including our finances.

Walking This Out...

One of the most important decisions my wife and I made when we were first married was to establish a budget and live on it. That decision has prevented conflict, protected our unity, and has kept us from the bondage of overwhelming debt.

In that budget, we committed to tithe and bring offerings as well. We have seen God's blessing as we've honored him with the firstfruits of our income.

We also determined that we would never carry a balance on our credit card. If we could not pay off the balance monthly, it was time to destroy the card.

It may seem archaic, but we still use envelopes for our cash needs. It is a simply visual lesson that when the envelope is empty, the spending stops. You don't spend what you don't have.

At least annually we review and renew our budget. When we encounter difficulties, we are not hesitant to get godly financial advice.

Finances are often a good barometer of our relational, emotional, and even spiritual condition. Over and over again I have seen where finances are in disarray, bigger issues are at the core.

Next Session

One of the greatest joys for any Christian is to lead someone to Christ. Fear fills the heart of some when they think about presenting the gospel to an unbeliever. They do not feel confident due to lack of training or lack of knowledge. In our next session we will consider several dynamic ways to share the good news of Jesus Christ with others.

Session 13

Contagious Faith

(Living out evangelism)

Jesus Said, "Go!"

Matthew 9:35-38: "And Jesus was going about all the cities and villages, teaching in their synagogues, and proclaiming the gospel of the kingdom, and healing every kind of disease and every kind of sickness. And seeing the multitudes, he felt compassion for them, because they were distressed and downcast like sheep without a shepherd. Then he said to his disciples, 'The harvest is plentiful, but the workers are few, therefore beseech the Lord of the harvest to send out workers into his harvest.'"

There are millions of people on planet earth who do not know Jesus Christ. Some of those people live around you. Are you willing to be a "harvest worker" to see those who are distressed and downtrodden come into the glorious kingdom of God?

Why is it that the harvest is so plentiful and the workers are so few? Let's consider a few reasons for the deficiency in the workforce.

1. We are so busy working in the grain elevator that we don't have time to make it out to the fields. The vast majority of our Christian life revolves around church and activities with other Christians. Association with other Christians is essential, but if it keeps us from the harvest fields, we have missed a portion of God's plan.

What percentage of your time is spent with non-Christians?

2. We've lost a "harvest team" mentality. We see ourselves in competition with other churches or denominations rather than as a team working together to bring in the harvest. That competitive spirit kills the effectiveness of our witness and work.

My student pastorate was in a small rural church in eastern Kansas. Wheat harvest was always a great event in that area. Because every available man was needed, I worked at the grain elevator during the harvest. I saw Farmer Brown help Farmer Smith get in his wheat, then they moved over and got all of Farmer Brown's wheat harvested. It was very much a team effort since the harvest was plentiful, and the season so critical. We must be a team again as the Body of Christ to see adequate laborers for the harvest.

3. We are so burdened with our own problems that we have little time or energy to labor in the harvest fields. When Jesus sent the disciples out in pairs to proclaim the kingdom, he told them to travel light (Luke 10:4). We are so encumbered with debt, work load, social commitments, chores at home, and so forth that we are not free to go out to share.

4. We've lost compassion for the lost. Do we really care that those unsaved people around us will spend an eternity in hell? Jesus was motivated by compassion to heal, deliver from demons, and proclaim the good news of salvation. A heart of compassion will propel us out into the harvest fields.

To what degree do you have a heart of compassion for those who do not know Christ?

5. Sin has crippled the effectiveness of many potential laborers. Because we struggle with bondage to some sin, it is difficult for us to proclaim effectively the good news of new life.

* * *

I knew a youth pastor who was secretly plagued with drunkenness. One night two of his teens saw him walking out of a liquor store with a case of beer. From that night on that youth pastor no longer had a voice with those teens, nor any other teens in that community. His sin disqualified him from effective service. I am glad to report that later that youth pastor did repent, did overcome his bondage to alcohol, and now is powerfully proclaiming the good news in the harvest field.

* * *

6. Jesus said that we needed to "beseech the Lord of the harvest to send out workers into his harvest." Perhaps the workers are few because we have not been "beseeching" enough! Could it be that God is looking to his people to become aroused enough about the lost to pray? Could it be that when we passionately pursue the Lord of the harvest to send out laborers that he will respond by passing out marching orders on the hearts of laborers?

7. Fear holds many of us back from the fields. I always pray when I go out doing door-to-door evangelism. The problem is, I sometimes pray that no one will be home! We feel inadequate, lacking knowledge, personality, or spiritual empowerment to lead another to Christ. "God has not given us a spirit of timidity, but of power and love and discipline" (2 Timothy 1:7). Even though we know God is with us and his Spirit will guide us, we still let fear hold us back.

Talk about a time when fear held you back from sharing Christ with another.

Evangelism Jesus Style

Matthew 9:35: "Jesus was going about all the cities and villages, teaching in their synagogues, and proclaiming the gospel of the kingdom, and healing every kind of disease and every kind of sickness."

Doing evangelism is not that tough! We simply follow in the footsteps of Jesus, telling good news and ministering to needs. Reaching out came naturally to Jesus, flowing from his huge heart of compassion. As those who are his, filled with his Spirit, we will reflect his character, care, and conviction to a lost world.

Contagious Christianity

Acts 2:47: "And the Lord was adding to their number day by day those who were being saved."

Acts 5:14: "And all the more believers in the Lord, multitudes of men and women, were constantly added to their number."

God blessed the early church with tremendous growth. It seems clear that a real key to the fruitful harvest was that folks couldn't keep the good news to themselves. They were so excited about Jesus, it wasn't a matter of feeling like, "Well, I should be out witnessing." It was a situation where people could not help but tell the good news.

Jesus said, "The things that proceed out of the mouth come from the heart" (Matthew 15:18). The early Christians had hearts so full of Jesus that they couldn't help but speak of him.

* * *

When I was in college I worked at a first-rate shoe store that sold only expensive shoes. I had bought my shoes at a discount shoe store down the street because as a college kid, I could not afford the shoes in this store even with my discount. I was having trouble selling shoes. In fact, I was sending people down the street to the discount place.

My boss called me in one day and said, "Daryl, you're not selling many shoes. What's the problem?"

I replied, "Our shoes are so expensive!"

He went into a lecture on the quality of our shoes

and then he said, "Have you ever tried on a pair of our shoes?"

I had not. My boss pulled out a pair of our dress shoes in my size. He slipped those shoes on my feet and I thought my feet were in heaven. I walked around feeling like I was floating on air. I felt support I did not know shoes could give. My boss gave me that pair of shoes.

I soon became top salesman. I couldn't help but tell people what a good thing I had found.

* * *

It seems to me that if we fully realize who Jesus is and all that he has done for us, we will be so full of him, he will spill out of our lives every day.

Is your faith contagious? Explain your answer.

Relational Evangelism

Luke 19:1-5: "And he entered and was passing through Jericho. And behold, there was a man called by the name of Zacchaeus; and he was a chief tax gatherer, and he was rich. And he was trying to see who Jesus was, and he was unable because of the crowd, for he was small in stature. And he ran on ahead and climbed up into a sycamore tree in order to see him, for he was about to pass through that way. And when Jesus came to the place, he looked up and said to him, 'Zacchaeus, hurry and come down, for today I must stay at your house.' "

Jesus was very much a "people person." He never saw a person as a project or merely as a target of evangelistic outreach. He genuinely cared about individuals. I love this short story about Zacchaeus. Jesus singled him out of a crowd, he called him by name, and then he went to his house for lunch. Jesus said, "Today salvation has come to this house!" Zacchaeus became a believer and a follower of Christ because of the authentic care Jesus had for him.

Evangelism at its best flows from relationship. While crusades, television ministries, street witnessing... even facebook posts and tweets all have their place in reaching people for Christ, the most effective means of reaching the world is to reach out to those nearest you. Be willing to build relationships with people who do not know Christ.

* * *

> Years ago I had a family as neighbors who did not know Christ. We both lived near the church building where I served. Each Sunday as I walked to services, I would wave to them. Often I would drop by and just chat. I went fishing with the father and his four sons. A deep friendship grew. I had the opportunity of leading the entire family to Christ. The father said to me some time after his conversion, "Daryl, I'm a Christian today because you were willing to be my friend and you never shoved Christianity down my throat."

* * *

While relational evangelism takes time, the time is a tremendous investment in the kingdom of God. Look for opportunities to build bridges of love, to reach those whom God has put around you. Genuinely care for them and sow seeds of good news into their lives and leave the rest up to God.

Seeking To Save By Serving

Mark 8:1-9: "In those days again, when there was a great multitude and they had nothing to eat, he called his disciples and said to them, 'I feel compassion for the multitude because they have remained with me now three days, and have

164

nothing to eat; and if I send them away hungry to their home, they will faint on the way; and some of them have come from a distance.' And his disciples answered him, 'Where will anyone be able to find enough to satisfy these men with bread here in a desolate place?' And he was asking them, 'How many loaves do you have?' And they said, 'Seven.' And he directed the multitude to sit down on the ground; and taking the seven loaves, he gave thanks and broke them, and started giving them to his disciples to serve to them, and they served them to the multitude. They also had a few small fish; and after he had blessed them, he ordered these to be served as well. And they ate and were satisfied; and they picked up seven large baskets full of what was left over of the broken pieces. And about four thousand were there; and he sent them away."

Jesus was always serving. His willingness to serve provided a platform for powerful evangelism. He did not serve so that he could do evangelism. He served out of compassion. Evangelism was a natural by-product of his compassionate service because Jesus cared deeply about both the body and the soul of the recipient of his love.

We too have constant opportunities to serve. It is a hurting, frustrated, and confused world in which we live. Like Jesus, we can mend the brokenhearted, bring hope to the downcast, feed the hungry, and minister healing and help to the weary and sick. Out of compassion we reach out with both a helping hand and the wonderful truth of the gospel. Look for those opportunities to serve. Give that cup of cold water in Jesus' name and just see what God does with the seed that is sown.

What service opportunities can you think of that you can do as an individual?

So What About Evangelism Programs/Methods?

I have met many Christians who are repulsed by the thought of using some prepared instrument to do evangelism. They resist an outlined approach to presenting the gospel. Can it possibly be sincere if it is a memorized speech? Wouldn't it be more effective just to share your heart?

Evangelism must be genuine and compassionate. It must flow from the heart. But sincerity does not require that we must do all things impromptu. I always spend hours of prayerful preparation before preaching a sermon, but I guarantee you that what I share from the pulpit, though somewhat rehearsed (yes, I do practice what I preach), is genuine and full of passion.

There are many good tools for evangelistic work. Check out the web or visit your local Christian bookstore and look for tracts and booklets designed for a simple presentation of the gospel message.

It is also helpful, if not imperative, that you have a grasp of a significant pool of scriptures related to salvation if you endeavor to lead someone to Christ. Remember, it is the truth that sets people free (John 8:32), not your opinions about Christ or your emotions about what he has done.

Don't be afraid to have some sort of evangelistic tool as you seek to reach out. Experience has shown me that men who have no method or plan for doing evangelism lead very few, if any, to Christ.

Do you have an evangelistic tool or method that you use in sharing the gospel with others?

How many people have you led to Christ?
     1-5   6-10   11-15   16-20   21-25   More

In Conclusion

One of the most exciting things for every Christian to be involved in is evangelism! Just as the angels rejoice when one sinner comes to know the Lord, so our heart rejoices when we have the privilege of introducing someone to Jesus Christ. Don't let fear or feelings of inadequacy stand in your way. God will go with you and will empower you to be a harvest worker.

If you lack compassion for the lost, pray that God will stir it up in you. If you lack boldness to witness the good news to others, seek the strength that God will give. You can do all things through Christ who strengthens you. The harvest is ready... pray that God will send out the laborers... and let one of those laborers be you!

Walking This Out...

I do not have the gift of evangelism. I have been around people who do and I have noticed that giftedness. But that does not excuse me from doing evangelism nor does it give me permission to have a calloused heart toward the lost.

I've committed hours learning how to do evangelism effectively, reading dozens of helpful books. (Many you will find in the resources appendix.) Men, continue to be students of evangelism. I've also walked carefully through the scriptures watching how Jesus reached out. He is our model.

I pray that God will help me to see lost people like he sees lost people. I ask him to enlarge my heart to love as he loves.

I am resolved to practice authentic faith 24/7 with a heart to "make Jesus look good" wherever I go. I pray for divine appointments to present the good news of the kingdom of God.

Because I believe faith is caught more than it is taught, I simply desire to live as an infectious Christian. With what I've learned from those with the gift of evangelism, I'm growing more and more effective at being a vessel God uses to draw people to himself.

Next Session

Our next session is our final session. We are going to consider specifically what is involved in discipling or mentoring another man. You will receive a list of resources for training up a new believer, as well as resources for further study on the topics we have discussed in our fourteen sessions together. Are you ready to walk out the Great Commission of Christ? "Go... make disciples!"

Session 14

Men Mentoring Men

(Making disciples)

Making Disciples

Matthew 28:18-20: "And Jesus came up and spoke to them, saying, 'All authority has been given to me in heaven and on earth. Go therefore and make disciples of all the nations, baptizing them in the name of the Father and the Son and the Holy Spirit, teaching them to observe all that I commanded you; and lo, I am with you always, even to the end of the age.' "

These are some of the final words of Jesus just before he ascended to heaven. Jesus issued a mandate to all who profess to be his disciples. He told us to be about the business of disciple-making. How thrilling to be a part of Christ's great plan for the human race. We have the joy of being God's instrument to introduce others to the person of Jesus Christ so that believing in him they might have everlasting life. We have the privilege to model and proclaim the principles of the kingdom of God that Jesus Christ lived and taught. Making disciples was a life priority for Jesus Christ — and as those who are his disciples, let's make it our priority too.

Before You Start

As you begin the great adventure of discipling or mentoring another man, consider the words of Jesus in his final marching orders to his disciples. "All authority has been given to me in heaven and on earth" (Matthew 28:18). He sends us out in his authority. Making disciples is not just a good idea, it is a God idea. It is not an invention of the human intellect, but is birthed from the heart of Christ himself. We do not make disciples in our frail human will or strength, but in the powerful authority of Jesus Christ.

* * *

> When I was in college, living in the dormitory, we
> had some rowdy guys down the hall who constant-
> ly made noise. I asked them several times to quiet
> down so that those who wanted to study could. They
> ignored me. The next semester I was sanctioned as
> a Resident Assistant by the President's office of the
> university. I was issued the responsibility and given
> the authority to maintain order in the dormitory. I ap-
> proached the same rowdy young men with a request
> for quiet with the word "STAFF" imprinted upon my
> shirt. They quickly complied. Authority made a great
> difference!

* * *

When you mentor another in the life and principles of the Christian
faith, you have the authority of Jesus Christ behind you. Remember,
he commissioned you. You are not calling men to obey you, but to
obey Christ. You are not merely presenting your opinions about life.
You are proclaiming profound biblical principles of the ways and
will of God. Responsibility and authority rest upon you as a result of
both the origin of your orders and the content of your presentation.

Another thing to remember as you begin is that as you gather with
another man or with several men, Jesus Christ is in your midst. He
said, "Lo, I am with you always, even to the end of the age" (Matthew 28:20). He promised that where two or more are gathered in
his name, he is there in the midst of them (Matthew 18:20).

Not only does Christ give us authority for mentoring men, he gives
us his very presence and power. Men will be transformed by the
revelation of the biblical truths and by the reality of Christ's person.
He will meet with you, and all involved will grow.

Ready... Set... Go!

Matthew 28:19: "Go, therefore, and make disciples..."

Jesus pursued men to mentor. He chose the twelve disciples in whom he would invest his life and teachings. While mentoring clearly is a two-way growing process and can be upon the request of the one wanting to be mentored, it is appropriate to pursue men to mentor. Observe and approach men whom you sense the Spirit of God prompting you to disciple. Avail yourself to them with a servant's heart to assist in their growth as Christian men.

As you consider men to mentor, the primary quality to look for is desire. Does the man want to grow? He may have a number of character flaws, struggles with sin, or ignorance of biblical truths; but if he has a desire to grow, you have a prime candidate for discipleship.

As you pursue the discipling relationship, make it workable for the other men to meet with you. Make yourself available to the man or men whom God has put upon your heart to mentor. Meet for breakfast, lunch, or perhaps of an evening on a regular basis. There is value in making your meeting times convenient, yet requiring some sacrifice on the part of you and the ones being discipled. Discipleship does require commitment and faithfulness.

As you conclude this course, pursue a mentoring relationship with another man or men. Do not sit and wait for some man to come to you. Jesus said, "Go!"

Are there men who come to mind that you might mentor now?

Is Baptism A Part Of This?

Matthew 28:19: "Baptizing them in the name of the Father and the Son and the Holy Spirit."

Jesus' disciples baptized new disciples. In John's gospel it says,

"Although Jesus himself was not baptizing, but his disciples were" (John 4:2). When Philip led the eunuch to Christ as recorded in Acts 8, he baptized him in a pool of water by the Gaza Road. Saul was baptized immediately after his conversion experience while staying at the home of Simon (Acts 9:18). Cornelius and his household were baptized right after the Holy Spirit had been imparted to them (Acts 10:47). Baptism is a key ingredient at the inception of a discipling relationship.

There are differing understandings as to when baptism should occur, how and upon whom it should be administered, and who has authority to baptize. Consult your pastor on this issue and submit to his counsel.

The real issue of baptism is what it demonstrates. It is a picture of surrender. The Apostle Paul wrote in Romans 6:4, "Therefore we have been buried with him through baptism into death, in order that as Christ was raised from the dead through the glory of the Father, so we too might walk in newness of life." Baptism depicts our dying to self in Christ and being raised in him to walk in new life. As you encounter men to disciple, call them to full surrender to Christ.

It's Time To Teach

Matthew 28:20: "... teaching them to observe all that I commanded you."

A major role in the mentoring process is teaching or instruction. Jesus seized every opportunity to present the principles of the kingdom of God. He taught in the synagogues, in the marketplace, on the seashore, in the wheat fields, and on the hilltops. The world was his classroom with the substance and circumstances around him as his tools of illustration.

Jesus constantly expounded upon the scriptures, taking matters past the letter of the law to issues of the heart. While he called people to repentance and strict adherence to the principles of the kingdom, he also proclaimed the merciful forgiveness and grace of God. He introduced the potential of abundant life to every aspect of our existence. He gave practical wisdom to the day in, day out encounters we all face. Jesus was a great teacher on God's kingdom principles of life, and so we too can be.

When you commit to mentor other men, do not merely meet together and discuss current affairs. Teach them to observe the commandments of Christ. Be diligent to present the word of God as a steady diet for the one you are discipling, for that will be true food for his spiritual nourishment.

As you teach the Bible, use contemporary, understandable illustrations to assist the one being discipled in the application of the word. Do not be afraid to use examples out of your own life to illustrate biblical truths — even your failures.

In these sessions of *Men Mentoring Men* we have considered biblical principles for many key areas of life. This is a good starting place in your mentoring relationship. You will find an appendix at the end of this course giving suggested resources for further study on each of the topics we have discussed. You will also find a list of tools specifically designed for mentoring another person. You may want to consider a simple Bible study course upon the completion of *Men Mentoring Men*.

Disciple Making As Jesus Did

> **Mark 3:13-14:** "And he went up to the mountain and summoned those whom he himself wanted, and they came to him. And he appointed twelve, that they might be with him, and that he might send them out to preach."

There were aspects to the mentoring that Jesus imparted that went beyond teaching. As we mentor other men, let's consider the pattern of Jesus who has set the example for us.

175

1. He was with them: Jesus spent time, not only with these twelve men, but with many who were his disciples. He walked with them and ate with them. His relationship far exceeded a mere teaching role. He was their companion and friend. Mentoring that produces fruitful life-change will flow from genuine care and friendship. Be willing to spend quality time with whomever God calls you to disciple.

What kind of time will you commit to those whom you will mentor?

2. He challenged them: Jesus not only stretched his disciples with the principles he taught, he challenged them with the life he called them to live. In an "eye for an eye," get-revenge culture, he called them to forgive. In the midst of a power-hungry humanity, he challenged them to be humble servants. He washed their feet and commanded them to do the same. Do not hesitate to challenge those whom you disciple. Christianity often is not easy or comfortable. Being a disciple of Jesus does have costs that must be counted. Call men to obey all that Christ has commanded.

3. Jesus was a constant example: Some of the best sermons Jesus gave had few or no words. When he touched the outcast repulsive leper with his healing hands of compassion, the disciples learned the lesson of mercy and love. As he chatted with the Samaritan woman by the well, the disciples saw the walls of prejudice crumble. Washing their feet in the upper room spoke volumes to his disciples about humility and servitude. Be an example to those whom you disciple. Do not merely teach Christian principles. Live them.

Give an example of a way you can model Christian principles to one whom you disciple.

4. Jesus prayed for his disciples: Jesus spoke powerful words recorded in Luke's gospel: "Simon, Simon, behold, Satan has demanded permission to sift you like wheat; but I have prayed for you, that your faith may not fail; and you, when once you have turned again, strengthen your brothers" (Luke 22:31-32). Sometime read the beautiful prayer of Jesus recorded in John 17, in which he prayed for his disciples and for us. Be faithful to pray for your disciples. Ask about their prayer needs and remember to follow up on the results of prayers.

5. Jesus held his disciples accountable to the kingdom principles he proclaimed: He often asked probing questions to encourage his disciples to stay on course. When many of Christ's disciples began to withdraw from him, he turned to the twelve and said, "You do not want to go away also, do you?" (John 6:66-67). The disciples renewed their commitment to follow Jesus. What a pointed question Jesus posed as his disciples slept in the garden: "So, you men could not keep watch with me for one hour?" (Matthew 26:40). Jesus often challenged and called his disciples to account because accountability helped keep his disciples on track.

Out of your relationship of friendship and trust, give one another permission to ask probing accountability questions. Knowing that someone is going to ask us to give account for our thoughts or actions is often enough motivation to keep us on course.

In Conclusion

You have in your heart a challenge and in your hand a tool. Will you go and make disciples? Find some men who want to grow and commit to be a mentor for them. Jesus has given his authority, his command, and his very presence for the call to discipleship. Be encouraged. You will do well in the power of Jesus Christ. You can do all things through Christ who strengthens you (Philippians 4:13)! Join the exciting adventure of making an eternal difference by making disciples!

Walking This Out...

As you wrap up the fourteen sessions of *Men Mentoring Men*, you should already have an idea of where you are headed next. Mentoring men is not a course you complete. It is a life of making disciples you live.

Sometimes I turn right around and launch into a new group working through *Men Mentoring Men*. More often, however, we stay together longer, either moving to *Men Mentoring Men, Again* or another book, or an inductive Bible Study.

I'm actually engaged in several groups, each at different stages of development. Don't see mentoring as a program or a course to complete, but as an opportunity to build discipling relationships for a lifetime.

And finally, I encourage the men who I have mentored to mentor other men. Second Timothy 2:2 is a life verse for me:

> "What you have heard from me in the presence of many witnesses entrust to faithful men who will be able to teach others also."

Faithful man, go! Make disciples!

Resources for Further Study

9Marks/Building Healthy Churches. Retrieved from www.9marks. org.

24-7 Prayer International. Retrieved from www.24-7prayer.com.

Aldrich, J.C. *Gentle Persuasion*.

Barna, G. *Encouraging Good Stewardship*.

Batterson, M. *Draw the Circle*.

Bennett, D. and Rita Bennett. *The Holy Spirit and You*.

Blackaby, H.T. and Claude King. *Experiencing God*.

Boschman, L. *Real Men Worship*.

Brain, P. *Go the Distance*.

Burkett, L. *The Complete Guide to Managing Your Money*.

Burkett, L. *Your Finances in Changing Times*.

Caldwell Ryrie, C. *You Mean the Bible Teaches That*.

Chambers, O. *My Utmost for His Highest*.

Cole, E.L. *Maximized Manhood*.

Coleman, R.E. *The Master Plan of Evangelism*.

Colson, C. *The Body*.

Comfort, R. *The Way of the Master*.

Cornwall, J. *Elements of Worship*.

Cornwall, J. *Heart of a Worshipper*.

Crabb, L.J. *The Marriage Builder*.

Crown Financial Ministries. Retrieved from www.crown.org.

Dawson, J. *Taking Our Cities For God*.

Desiring God. Retrieved from www.desiringgod.org.

Dobson, J. *Love for a Lifetime*.

Evans, T. *No More Excuses.*

Ezzo, G. and Anne Marie Ezzo. *Growing Kids God's Way.*

Family Life Today. Retrieved from www.familylife.com.

Farrar, S. *Point Man.*

Fay, B. *Share Jesus Without Fear.*

Fee, G.D. *God's Empowering Presence.*

Focus on the Family. Retrieved from www.focusonthefamily.org.

Forster, P. *For Instruction in Righteousness.*

Foster, R. *Treasury of Christian Discipline.*

Fullam, E. *Living the Lord's Prayer.*

Glass, L. *The Church Reigning Through Intercession.*

Gothard, B. *Training Faithful Men.*

Graham, B. *The Holy Spirit.*

Harley Jr., W.F. *His Needs — Her Needs.*

Hauck, G. *Is My Church What God Meant It to Be?*

Healthy Church Network, The. Retrieved from www.healthychurch-network.com.

Hicks, R. *The Masculine Journey.*

Holy Spirit Facts, The. Retrieved from www.theholyspirit.com.

Houston, J. *The Heart's Desire.*

Hughes, R.K. *Disciplines of a Godly Man.*

Hughes, R.K. *Acts: The Church Afire.*

Internet Accountability. Retrieved from www.covenanteyes.com.

Jeremiah, Dr. D. *Turning Point Ministries.* Retrieved from www. davidjeremiah.org.

Kaiser, D. Bruce & Brauch. *Hard Sayings of the Bible.*

LaHaye, T. *How to Study the Bible for Yourself.*

LaHaye, T. *Spirit Controlled Temperament.*

Lewis, C.S. *Mere Christianity.*

Lindsell, H. *The Battle for the Bible.*

Lucado, M. *In the Grip of Grace.*

Lucado, M. *Upwords.* Retrieved from www.maxlucado.com.

Man in the Mirror. Retrieved from www.maninthemirror.org.

McCartney, B., editor. *What Makes A Man.*

McDonald, J. *Walk in the Word*. Retrieved from www.OnePlace.com.

McDowell, J. *The Father Connection*.

McGee, R. *The Search for Significance*.

McGee, J.V. *Thru The Bible*. Retrieved from www.thruthebible.org.

Morley, P. *I Surrender*.

Morley, P. *The Man in the Mirror*.

National Prayer Center, The. Retrieved from www.prayer.ag.org.

Ogilvie, L.J. *Praying With Power*.

Ortiz, J.C. *Call to Discipleship*.

Peale, R.S. *Secrets of Staying in Love*.

Pinnock, C.H. *Flame of Love*.

Pippert, R.M. *Out of the Salt Shaker*.

Proctor, W. and R. Theodore Benna. *Escaping the Coming Retirement Crisis*.

Promise Keepers. Retrieved from www.promisekeepers.org.

Pure Life (Sexual addictions). Retrieved from www.purelifeministries.org.

Reimer, K. *1001 Ways to Introduce Your Child to God*.

Ron Blue. Retrieved from www.masteryourmoney.com.

Rosberg, G. *Focus on the Family: Guard Your Heart*.

Servant Evangelism. Retrieved from www.servantevangelism.com.

Sjogren, S. *Conspiracy of Kindness*.

Smalley, G. *Making Love Last Forever*.

Sorge, B. *Exploring Worship*.

Sproul, R.C. *Knowing Scripture*.

Swindoll, C.R. *Man to Man*.

Swindoll, L. *Wide My World, Narrow My Bed*.

Thomas, R. *After the Spirit Comes*.

Tillapaugh, F.R. *Unleashing the Church*.

Wagner, C.P. *Finding Your Spiritual Gifts*.

Walling, J. *Daring to Dance With God*.

Warren, R. *The Purpose Driven Church*.

Way of the Master Training. Retrieved from www.wayofthemaster. com.

Webber, R. *Authentic Worship in a Changing Culture.*

Wheat, Dr. E. *Intended for Pleasure.*

Wheat, Dr. E. *Secret Choices.*

White, J. *Looking for Love in All the Wrong Places.*

White, T.B. *The Believer's Guide to Spiritual Warfare.*

Willhite, B.J. *Why Pray?*

Worship Network. Retrieved from www.worship.net.

Yorkey, M., editor. *Growing A Healthy Family.*

Bible Study Resources

Books

LaHaye, T. *How to Study the Bible for Yourself.*
Lindsell, H. *The Battle for the Bible.*
Sproul, R.C. *Knowing Scripture.*

Commentaries

Harris, R., editor. *The Complete Biblical Library.*
Ogilvie, L.J., editor. *The Communicator's Commentary.*
Walvoord, J. and Roy B. Zuck, editors. *The Bible Knowledge Commentary.*

Study Bibles

Barker, K., editor. *The NIV Study Bible.*
Hayford, J.W., editor. *Spirit Filled Life Bible.*
New King James Version.
Ryrie, C.C., commentator. *The Ryrie Study Bible.*

Dictionaries/Concordances

Strong, J. *Strong's Exhaustive Concordance.*
Unger, M.F. *Unger's Bible Dictionary.*

Note: There are so many great Bible apps. Good to consult with your pastor as to reliability and compatible theology. I love Bible Gateway.

CPSIA information can be obtained
at www.ICGtesting.com
Printed in the USA
FFOW03n1450040314
4010FF